WARRIOR • 133

SOE AGENT

Churchill's Secret Warriors

TERRY CROWDY   ILLUSTRATED BY STEVE NOON

First published in Great Britain in 2008 by Osprey Publishing,
PO Box 883, Oxford, OX1 9PL, UK
PO Box 3985, New York, NY 10185-3985, USA
Email: info@ospreypublishing.com

Osprey Publishing is part of the Osprey Group.

Transferred to digital print on demand 2013

First published 2008
1st impression 2008

Printed and bound by PrintOnDemand-Worldwide.com, Peterborough, UK

A CIP catalogue record for this book is available from the British Library

ISBN: 978 1 84603 276 9

Page layout by Mark Holt
Index by Bob Munro
Typeset in Sabon and Myriad Pro
Originated by PDQ Digital Media Solutions Ltd, Bungay, UK

Glossary

Abwehr	German military intelligence organization
Feldgendarmerie	German military police
Gestapo (*Geheimestaatspolizei*)	Nazi secret state police force
Kripo (*Kriminalpolizei*)	Nazi criminal detective agency
Milice	French fascist paramilitary force raised in 1943 to counter resistance groups
SD (*Sicherheitsdienst*)	Security Service of the SS
Sipo (*Sicherheitspolizei*)	Nazi security police; formed of the Gestapo and Kripo
SS (*Schutzstaffel*)	lit. 'protection squad'; military wing of Nazi Party

Artist's note

Readers may care to note that the original paintings from which the colour plates in this
book were prepared are available for private sale. The Publishers retain all reproduction
copyright whatsoever. All enquiries should be addressed to:

Steve Noon,
50 Colchester Avenue,
Penylan,
Cardiff CF23 9BP,
UK

The Publishers regret that they can enter into no correspondence upon this matter.

Imperial War Museum Collections

Many of the photos in this book come from the Imperial War Museum's huge collections
which cover all aspects of conflict involving Britain and the Commonwealth since the start
of the twentieth century. These rich resources are available online to search, browse and
buy at www.iwmcollections.org.uk. In addition to Collections Online, you can visit the
Visitor Rooms where you can explore over 8 million photographs, thousands of hours of
moving images, the largest sound archive of its kind in the world, thousands of diaries and
letters written by people in wartime, and a huge reference library. To make an appointment,
call (020) 7416 5320, or e-mail: mail@iwm.org.uk.

Imperial War Museum www.iwm.org.uk

The Woodland Trust

Osprey Publishing is supporting the Woodland Trust, the UK's leading woodland
conservation charity, by funding the dedication of trees.

www.ospreypublishing.com

CONTENTS

SOE AGENT – CHURCHILL'S SECRET WARRIORS

SOE team in Crete, June 1944, sporting a variety of standard SOE weapons, including a 'Tommy' gun (left) and commando knife (centre). The figure of the left is Corporal Steve Gillespie, the group's radio operator. To blend in he has adopted the native custom of growing a beard and wearing his hair in plaits. In areas where German control was strongest, it was imperative that SOE agents adapted themselves to local costume. (IWM HU66047)

INTRODUCTION

Resistance to Nazi occupation was inevitable given the brutal and exploitative manner with which Germany treated the conquered territories. Whatever claims Nazi propaganda made about a new world order, one of latter-day Teutonic knights saving Europe from the evils of Bolshevism, evidence on the ground told a different story. Innocent civilians were persecuted, rounded up, incarcerated and murdered for reasons of race and creed, regardless of age or gender. The wealth of the conquered nations was bled: finance, industry and manpower were swallowed by the Nazi war machine. Free speech was stifled, political dissent crushed, curfews were imposed, movement restricted, food was rationed and with shortages of every kind, misery abounded on a scale not seen in Europe since the days of the Black Death. Unlike previous

occupations, Nazi control was like a virus, intent on infiltrating every level of human existence and perverting it for its own satisfaction. With their governments scattered and armed forces bested in the field, the occupied peoples waited in quiet discontent for a show of leadership.

Before June 1941, when Hitler invaded the Soviet Union, there was one beacon of hope for the people of Europe. Hitler had tried to reason with the British. He had tried to smash their cities from the air and starve them with U-boat blockade. Somehow he failed. Prime Minister Winston Churchill had seen the evil inherent in Nazism and determined to face it down, come what may. He made it quite clear that even if invaded, the British would not roll over. They would fight for every brick. London, he said, was so large it could swallow a German army if it dared to attack.

Galvanizing as Churchill was, the war would not be won with rhetoric. After the retreat from Dunkirk and the fall of France, there was no chance of a British army returning to the Continent in strength. Nor in 1940 was Bomber Command ready to take the war into the German heartland. Beyond the pinpricks of occasional commando raids, something more was needed. Britain thought of ways to play on existing anti-Nazi sentiments to cause uprisings, stirring up trouble to the point at which Europe would become ungovernable. To do this the Minister of Economic Warfare, Hugh Dalton, was convinced a new organization should be created to go into occupied Europe and develop movements comparable to Sinn Fein in Ireland and the guerrillas that made Spain a nightmare for Napoleon's armies. The new weapons of war would be agitation, strikes, random acts of terror, propaganda and assassination. In this struggle for democratic survival, it really was a case of 'no holds barred'.

As such, the Special Operations Executive (SOE) was created in July 1940. Outside military control and independent of the Secret Intelligence Service (SIS), also known as MI6, SOE began recruiting and training agents to be sent into occupied Europe. In denting Germany's atom bomb project, assassinating Reinhard Heydrich (a leading architect of the Holocaust) and fostering innumerable resistance groups, the deeds of SOE rank among the most important of the war. Before descending by parachute, or coming ashore on a quiet, moonlit beach, the men and women of SOE were put through the most intense training then available. As unorthodox as it was tough, SOE's training course equipped agents with the necessary skills to survive behind enemy lines. Here we examine that training programme and reveal the key to the organization's success in the field.

When operating in areas only partially garrisoned by the Germans, many SOE agents opted to wear battledress uniform in order to 'fly the flag' and encourage local resistance groups. Here we see Major David Smiley operating in Albania, sporting local headdress with his battledress blouse. Note the pistol holster over the right thigh. (IWM HU65070)

CHRONOLOGY – SOE IN EUROPE

1938

30 September	Munich Agreement signed, Germany occupies part of Czechoslovakia
	British MI6 sets up D Section (sabotage)
	British General Staff forms research section GS(R) to investigate possibilities of guerrilla warfare

1939

Early May	GS(R) becomes Military Intelligence (Research) or MI(R)
	completion of Field Service Regulations for guerrilla warfare
1 September	Germany invades Poland
3 September	Britain and France declare war on Germany

1940

10 May	Churchill becomes Prime Minister of Britain
16 July	Churchill invites Hugh Dalton to take control of 'special operations'

1941

23 January	Operation *Rubble* – five Norwegian ships loaded with ball bearings taken from Gothenburg
25 February	first signal received from occupied Europe – agent Odd Starheim transmits from Norway
15 March	Operation *Savanna* – unsuccessful SOE plan to attack German Pathfinder squadron KG.100 in retaliation for the Blitz
5 May	first F Section agent (Georges Bégué) parachuted into France
7 June	successful attack on large electricity transformer station near Bordeaux by RF Section
4 September	first Lysander aircraft pick-up in France near Châteauroux
7 September	SOE infiltrates mining engineer Captain Hudson into Yugoslavia by submarine
20 October	SOE penetrates Crete
28 December	*Anthropoid* team lands in Czechoslovakia to assassinate Reinhard Heydrich

1942

6 March SOE radio operator Huub Lauwers arrested in The Hague; his set is successfully controlled by the Germans in Operation *North Pole*

27 May Heydrich assassinated in Prague

10 June Czech town of Lidice is destroyed in retaliation for Heydrich's assassination

18 June Heydrich's assassins killed in gun battle with German soldiers in Prague church

June supply drops to Greece for attacks on shipping; these attacks disrupt supplies to Germans in North Africa

19 October Operation *Grouse* – team of four SOE-trained Norwegian commandos begins mission to destroy heavy water plant at Vemork

19 November Operation *Freshman* – British gliders crash while bringing commando force to aid *Grouse* team

25 November *Harling* group destroys Gorgopotamos bridge in Greece, disrupting rail supplies to Afrika Korps

1943

16 February Operation *Gunnerside* – six more Norwegians dropped to aid *Grouse* team

23 February *Gunnerside* and *Grouse* teams link up

27/28 February successful attack on Vemork plant

21 June Gestapo arrest leading French resister, Jean Moulin, in Lyon; SOE receives a series of setbacks in France as arrests continue; ARCHDEACON circuit members arrested along with codes – their radio is successfully 'played-back' by the Germans until May 1944

18 September Fitzroy Maclean sent to Yugoslavia to act as Churchill's representative to Marshal Tito

October SOE agents infiltrated into northern Italy and Rome to support growing Italian partisan movement

5 November Peugeot sabotages its own factory after SOE arrange for RAF attacks to stop

31 November on Lake Tinnsjo, Norwegian agents sink ferry carrying remaining heavy water stocks to Germany

1944

1 April	Germans end Operation *North Pole* – of 56 agents sent to Holland, 43 were intercepted on landing
26 April	General Kreipe kidnapped by SOE agents on Crete
5 June	activation messages sent out to French resistance on BBC
6 June	Allied landings in Normandy – SOE-trained 'Jedburgh' teams parachute into France
8 June	2nd SS Panzer Division 'Das Reich' begins march from Toulouse to Normandy – faced with constant resistance attacks it takes two weeks to travel 450 miles (724km)
25/26 June	flight to retrieve V2 rocket plans from Polish resistance
1 August	Warsaw uprising begins – SOE's attempts to supply the city from Italian airfields offers only limited support; Stalin refuses to let them use Soviet airfields
25 August	liberation of Paris

1945

7 May	war ends in Europe

1946

15 January	SOE closed down – an undisclosed number of agents move to MI6

Cetnik partisans examine parachute containers of supplies dropped to them by Allied aircraft. Notice how the 'Type H' containers break down into a series of drums for easier handling. (IWM: HU57247)

FORMATION AND ORGANIZATION

As it became increasingly clear that German expansionism was likely to cause a war, the British Army and MI6 began independent experiments with the ideas of sabotage and subversion. Thus came into being MI6's D Section ('D' for destruction) and the War Office's Military Intelligence Research section, MI(R). Between them these two organizations created specialized training schools and drew up plans to interrupt the supply of vital raw materials to Germany. Economic warfare experts had pinpointed Germany's reliance on high-grade Swedish iron ore and Romanian oil. In the latter case, plans were drawn up to destroy the oil wells or at least disrupt barge traffic on the River Danube.

In addition to communication, one of SOE's principal roles was to supply resistance groups with weapons and equipment. Here we see a massive container drop somewhere over occupied Europe. Note the large number of parachutes already on the ground. (IWM HU32842)

By the end of May 1940, even before the Dunkirk debacle, there was a wide-ranging discussion on utilizing anti-Nazi resistance groups in occupied Europe. Everyone could see the need for a single organization to make this plan an operational reality, but there was little consensus on who should have ownership of the project. The War Office claimed it was best placed, as did the Foreign Office, which controlled MI6.

There was a third voice in the argument. The Minister for Economic Warfare, Hugh Dalton, pointed out that left-wing organizations should be used to shake off the Nazi yoke, as they were more experienced in the sort of agitation and propaganda required. As a left-wing politician himself, Dalton believed he was the natural choice to lead such an organization and, after much lobbying, he received the chairmanship. The Special Operations Executive (SOE) was given its charter on 22 July 1940, with Churchill famously telling Dalton to 'set Europe ablaze'. Although Churchill was at the opposite end of the political spectrum to Dalton, and is believed to have disliked him, the British prime minister was an enthusiastic supporter of the new organization. The head of MI6 was not. Irked that the new organization was not under its control, MI6 voiced concerns that SOE was staffed by amateurs who would make life intolerably difficult for their agents working in the same areas.

SOE was based at 64 Baker Street, London, and operated under the cover title 'Inter-Service Research Bureau'. In terms of size, at its peak SOE was the equivalent of a weak army division, with a little over 13,000 personnel, a quarter of whom were women. In terms of the number of agents produced by SOE, that question is more difficult to assess. The official history of SOE records that approximately 6,800 students were put through training courses by the organization. Only 480 of these students were British and 760 belonged to the American equivalent of SOE, the Office of Strategic Services (OSS). In his history of resistance in Europe, French historian Henri Michel gives the figure of 7,000 agents dropped into Europe. Given that not every British agent actually passed through SOE's school system, this figure may be close to the truth. Unfortunately no central record of agents was maintained; some agents were actually regular soldiers belonging to the armed forces of various governments-in-exile and went into Europe wearing commando

SOE requisitioned a number of workshops where it produced an array of secret gadgetry and equipment. Pictured here is the interior of the Bontex Knitting Works at Wembley, otherwise known as Station VIIa (wireless section). Other important establishments included Station IX (research and development) at The Frythe estate near Welwyn Garden City; Station XIV (forgery) at Briggens, Essex; and Station XV (camouflage) at The Thatched Barn in Borehamwood. (IWM HU56749)

uniforms. At the same time, an enormous number of resisters were recruited by SOE in the field and never actually set foot in Britain.

SOE is equally hard to pin down in terms of structure. It was a fluid organization, adapting to the demands of the war in different theatres. At the outset SOE was divided into three branches: SO1, SO2 and SO3. The first branch was an amalgamation of various propaganda organizations, including a section of the Foreign Office known as 'EH', after its base at Electra House in London. In time SO1 became an organization in its own right, known as the Political Warfare Executive (PWE) and therefore passes from the scope of this account. SO3 was theoretically a planning branch, but it never materialized into anything worthy of note and can similarly be discounted here. As for SO2, this was formed by amalgamating MI(R) and D Section. It was this branch that became the mainstay of SOE.

Like any branch of the Civil Service, SOE was divided up into a number of directorates and sections. At its height, these directorates included Intelligence, Signals, Finance and Supplies, under which came numerous research and production establishments. These research stations developed and provided the gadgets used by agents in the field, including everything from forged passports, silent pistols and wireless transmitters up to submersible vessels. The sharp end of the organization was the operational branch under the control of Major-General Colin Gubbins, formerly of MI(R). As the previous Osprey title *French Resistance Fighter* (Warrior 117) showed, SOE is most famous for supplying the Maquis in France and waging a sabotage campaign in support of the Normandy landings, but SOE had agents at work in Denmark, Norway, Holland, Italy, Greece and Crete, Yugoslavia, Czechoslovakia, Romania, Bulgaria, Albania, North Africa and

The Welman one-man submarine, developed in 1942 at Station IX as a reconnaissance craft. Typical of SOE's inventive spirit, the prototype was said to contain a seat from an Austin 7 motor car, the joystick of a crashed Spitfire and the motor from a London trolley bus. (IWM HU56768)

throughout the Far East. Each individual country was allocated a section responsible for recruiting agents who might be used in their area of responsibility. These sections were staffed by officers with an excellent knowledge of the country, its peoples and language. They were responsible for finding, recruiting, briefing, and controlling agents, as well as gathering intelligence and planning operations.

The country sections were further grouped by theatre or other logical chunks to form a number of groups looking after the various theatres of the war. The London Group covered France, Belgium, Holland, Scandinavia and Germany. The Mediterranean theatre was split into two groups: one in London that included the western Mediterranean, Italy, the Balkans and Central Europe, and more locally the Cairo Group, or Special Operations Mediterranean (SOM). The latter was divided in April 1944 as Force 266 (Yugoslavia, Albania) and Force 139 (Poland, Czechoslovakia). Two other groups covered the Far East and the Indian subcontinent respectively.

Another set of Station IX inventions: the Welbike – a collapsible motorcycle that could be fitted into a standard parachute container – and a generator for charging the batteries of a wireless set in the field. (IWM HU56740)

In more detail, France was split into five sections, each of which formed numerous 'circuits' or networks inside France. These varied in size quite wildly from a short-lived one-man show (TUTOR circuit), to enormous networks with thousands of members. The first was F Section (F for France), a politically neutral organization capable of acting with any group determined to fight Germans. RF Section (*République Française*) represented the provisional government of Général de Gaulle. On a smaller scale, EU/P Section (European Poles) dealt with the large number of Poles living in France at the time of the Nazi invasion. DF Section was responsible for running escape networks out of France and a fifth section known as AMF catered for the supporters of de Gaulle's rival, Général Giraud. This section was based in Algiers and conducted operations in the south of France. Also, in 1944 the 'Jedburgh' teams were created to act as uniformed liaison with resistance groups in France. The project was a joint one between SOE, OSS and de Gaulle's military intelligence agency, the *Bureau Central de Renseignements et d'Action* (Intelligence and Operations Central Bureau; BCRA). Each team had an American or British officer, a French officer and a radio operator.

AGENT SELECTION

The first problem facing SOE was finding recruits. SOE was a secret organization and it could not put up posters on a London bus asking for volunteers. Before the war began, MI(R) began building up a register of soldiers and civilians with the necessary qualifications for clandestine work. The system worked on personal and indirect recommendation. Many of those chosen came from the City: businessmen whose backgrounds afforded them cover and excuses to work abroad. Others were mining engineers, or journalists, all men who had worked abroad and had detailed knowledge of places like the Balkans or France. Some were serving soldiers with a second language – either from

SOE agent Jacqueline Nearne, seen here learning evasion techniques in the information film *Now It Can Be Told*. In 1944 the RAF Film Production Unit began documenting the activities of SOE using Nearne and fellow SOE agent Captain Harry Ree. With both having recently returned from occupied France, this film forms the most realistic pictorial demonstration of SOE agents in training. (IWM MH24434)

schooling or by dint of a foreign parent. When SOE came into being, MI(R) handed over an index card system naming 1,000 potential recruits.

SOE also trawled through the records identifying those people with dual nationality – an English father and a French mother, say. Although by preference SOE would have preferred to recruit only British nationals, it quickly recognized the importance of recruiting locals. During the war there was no lack of foreign refugees and servicemen in Britain. All foreign nationals coming into Britain had to pass through a reception centre in Wandsworth. Here everyone coming out of occupied Europe was vetted by the Security Service (MI5) to identify Nazi agents trying to enter the UK disguised as refugees. These arrivals formed a useful pool of potential recruits, but SOE came into conflict with the various governments-in-exile. who believed they had first claim over their countrymen's services. This was particularly so with de Gaulle's Free French. SOE was effectively barred from recruiting anyone arriving in the United Kingdom from France or from a French colony. These went to de Gaulle's Free French forces in London. Those with dual Anglo-French nationality or British passports were a different matter. A number of French-Canadians joined SOE, as did citizens from Mauritius, Madagascar, the Seychelles and Indo-China. There was also an unofficial recognition that Frenchmen recruited by SOE in France were also given up by de Gaulle.

Some attempt was made to recruit POWs. In April 1941 the so-called 'Yak Mission' left England to recruit anti-fascist Italians from among the POWs taken by General Wavell in Egypt. Headed by Captain Peter Fleming (brother of 'James Bond' author, Ian), Yak's goal was to recruit a thousand men for a 'Garibaldi legion' to spearhead an invasion of Italy. Despite visiting numerous POW cages around Cairo, not a single Italian volunteered.

There was more luck with German prisoners or deserters who were recruited and sent back to Germany as agents. The first of these was an anti-Nazi named Kuehnel, who was captured on a meteorological ship in June 1941. Arriving in Germany, he unfortunately vanished without trace and was never heard of again. The second attempt was only slightly more successful. In November 1942, deserter Kurt Koenig was recruited in Spain and trained by SOE. Parachuted onto the Dutch–German border on the night of 16 February 1943, he unfortunately overshot the drop zone and landed on the roof of a farmhouse where a wedding reception was in progress. Claiming he was an airman, he gave the wedding guests the slip and fled back to Spain.

Towards the later stages of the war, 54 German prisoners were recruited before being posted as POWs. Given over to X Section (Germany) they were nicknamed 'Bonzos'. Between November 1944 and April 1945, 19 Bonzos were sent into Germany on a variety of missions. Although none managed to establish radio communications, most of them survived and by their own accounts were not completely unsuccessful.

Perhaps the most marked difference between recruitment in SOE and the armed forces was that SOE was willing to send women to the frontline. (Although the 'he' pronoun is commonly used throughout this book, this is purely for grammatical reasons.) True enough, the majority of women in SOE were employed as clerks, drivers, telephonists and wireless operators, but the records show that 49 women were sent into France, 12 of whom met their end in Nazi concentration camps. Although female agents rarely carried out sabotage, they were vital as wireless operators and especially couriers. With most young men in occupied territories either held as POWs or enrolled into forced labour, young women did not attract the same level of attention when moving about town. Female agents were told the hazardous nature of what was being asked of them and what they might expect if captured, but they were encouraged to volunteer all the same.

The Interview

Once identified, potential agents were invited to an interview by the country section concerned. This would be conducted fairly informally and was a cat-and-mouse routine in which the interviewer tried to entice the interviewee into volunteering without actually giving away the job details. Using the example of F Section, the interview took place in what was described as a 'grimy' third-floor back bedroom of the Northumberland Hotel. Here SOE had commandeered room 321 and furnished it simply with a trestle table covered in green baize cloth and two rickety fold-away chairs. The interviewer, Selwyn Jepson, would switch the conversation from English to French. The key to the agent's survival in the field would be their ability to speak the local language fluently. It was not enough for an agent to say he spoke French – it was important he could speak the local dialect perfectly otherwise his accent would mark him as an outsider.

While testing the candidates' linguistic skills, Jepson would probe their character and form an opinion on their suitability. The characteristics of a saboteur, an organizer of partisans, or a clandestine radio operator were not the same as those of a regular soldier. This is not to say professional soldiers made bad students of secret warfare, but in many cases their talents were better suited elsewhere. Soldiering is in the most part a team game. Soldiers are taught to rely on their comrades and to place trust in their officers' instructions. Almost the exact reverse applied to the average SOE agent. Working behind enemy lines they were cautioned to trust no one and become self-reliant.

Soldiers are legitimized by their wearing of a uniform, which under international law gave them certain expectations if captured by the enemy. Agents without a uniform had no legal combatant status and were liable to be executed as spies, often after prolonged interrogation and torture. They were isolated, and constantly one step away from capture. Once behind enemy lines there was no safety valve of a spell of leave, and in the same way that long periods of boredom can affect soldiers' morale, the constant fear of capture, and the duplicity of living under an assumed identity, were powerful stressors that played on the nerves and exhausted even the best. Their vulnerability was highlighted by their inability to communicate with home. Agents could not tell their families what they were doing and had little prospect of sending or receiving news when on a mission. With these factors in mind, SOE had to be very careful that the agents they sent into action were capable of overcoming these psychological hazards.

Although there was no specific mould, SOE wanted discreet, level-headed candidates with the capacity to think and act aggressively. They did not want

THE INTERVIEW

As a secret organization, SOE could not openly recruit. Instead it relied on hours of research, looking for the right type of individual, or following up personal recommendations and delving into background checks. At the first interview the emphasis was on assessing the candidate's language skills. Later on, when the large partisan groups were formed and agents did not have to live in towns, the language stipulation was perhaps less stringent. In addition, more risks were taken with radio operators simply because there were not enough of them to go around. In most cases, the candidates went away from their first interview with only vague ideas of what they were getting drawn into, although sometimes others were told the risks up front and given a blunt 'take it or leave it' proposal. The gut feeling of the interviewer was what mattered most. Even if a negative report came from the scientific appraisal by the Student Assessment Board, this was often ignored in favour of the recommendation of the recruiting officer.

This photograph captures the adventurous spirit of SOE officers on their missions overseas. Here Colonel Bill Hudson makes a horseback reconnaissance of bridges selected for destruction in Yugoslavia. Notice the rifle-armed scout crouching on the hill below him. (IWM HU45083)

jilted, neurotic or psychopathic individuals with a chip on their shoulders. In the most part they should be young and fit, able to look after themselves in a fight and withstand the rigours of sleep deprivation and inclement weather. The head of F Section, Major Maurice Buckmaster, described successful recruits as having 'a rugged honesty and singleness of purpose' about them. Physique was less important as recruits could be knocked into shape on the training courses, but what they needed was 'guts' and the bravery to conquer fear.

If deemed suitable by the interviewer, the candidate would be told to go away and think about things for a week or so and come back for a second interview. At this point he or she would be told something more about the task in store. He was told he had only a 50/50 chance of coming back, but that the sacrifice would be worth it. In fact, the casualty rate among agents proved lower than feared and three-quarters survived. On balance, an SOE agent had a better chance of survival than if he had gone into Bomber Command.

After a third interview, the candidate would be formally accepted if all went well. To maintain his cover he would be enrolled in the armed forces. Candidates who were not already serving officers were immediately given the rank of second lieutenant and put on the army's General List or enrolled as officers in the Women's Auxiliary Air Force (WAAF). All candidates were now ready for one of the toughest training programmes of World War II.

THE TRAINING SYSTEM

Prospective agents were put through a rigorous training and assessment programme to gauge their suitability for field operations. Before agents were passed fit, they would have to complete three tiers of schooling, each designed to push them to the limits and prepare them for the dangerous work ahead. In outline, the students (prospective agents were always called students) would spend three to four weeks at a preliminary school before passing on to 'Group A', or 'paramilitary schools'. There the students would undergo a gruelling 3–5-week syllabus of physical exercise, fieldcraft and combat training. The students would then have an opportunity to gain their parachute wings at RAF Ringway before being sent on to 'Group B', or 'finishing schools' located around Lord Montagu's Beaulieu estate in the New Forest, Hampshire. The training became more psychologically demanding as the students were trained in spycraft, learning everything from using disguises to safe-breaking. When the Germans learned of this unorthodox syllabus through captured agents, they nicknamed Beaulieu 'the gangster school'. With the formal training complete, the agents might then be sent to a specialist school to receive additional one-to-one lessons. The most common specialist schools taught industrial sabotage or wireless operation. Once training was complete, the students would be handed back to their country section, which would take care of the agents before they were sent overseas.

There would normally be a mixture of nationalities on each course and ideally there would have been enough resources to supply adequate translators. Each country section would provide a conducting officer to help their students pass through the course. Some of the conducting officers were agents themselves, either recuperating from a mission or having retired from active operations. They shared the discomforts of the training course with their charges and offered advice and encouragement where needed. They also observed the student closely and reported any deficiencies in character that might not have been revealed at the interview stage.

Although many guessed what they were being trained for, the students were not told what they had volunteered for until they reached the Group B stage. Most of the training before that point was done under the guise of commando training. As an additional security precaution, students who dropped out or failed to meet SOE's vigorous needs were not sent back to their regiments or civilian life immediately. Although there was no stigma or accusations of cowardice for dropping out – some people were just not suited to clandestine life – SOE maintained a series of workshops at Inverlair where ex-students were detained for a period. Nicknamed 'the Cooler', the ex-students would be assigned tasks in the workshops, keeping them busy until it was felt that what they had learned of SOE would no longer compromise security. In total, there were about 50 training schools dotted throughout the British Isles, mostly contained in isolated country houses. This choice of venue led to claims that the initials S.O.E. stood for 'Stately 'omes of England'.

The three-tier training programme was developed by former MI(R) man Colonel 'Tommy' Davies, who used a syllabus largely based on a set of pre-war manuals on guerrilla warfare. These manuals had been developed by Colin Gubbins and had been issued as a Field Service Regulation in May 1939. Gubbins studied the history books for examples of guerrilla fighting and was inspired by the Spanish resistance against Napoleon, the example of Lawrence of Arabia, and his German contemporary, Wilhelm Wassmuss, who

A still from the RAF film showing a typical commando-type obstacle course used in the fitness training of SOE students. (IWM MH24432)

operated in Persia during World War I. Closer to home, Gubbins studied examples of agitation and uprising from within the British Empire: in South Africa, Palestine, the North-West Frontier of India, and also Ireland, where he had served during the Anglo-Irish War (1920–21). The tactics of the irregular Irish Republican Army (IRA) formed a particularly useful example for Gubbins to work on.

Gubbins' research resulted in the production of three pamphlets. The first was entitled *The Art of Guerrilla Warfare* and set out some basic tenets. The key to guerrilla warfare was strong, charismatic leadership, the goodwill of the local population and the submachine gun. The latter was a particularly important departure from regular fighting techniques. Guerrilla fighting generally took place at close range and was not prolonged. The person that could fire the most shots quickest had the advantage – as any Chicago mobster worth his salt could attest. Part two of the series was called *The Partisan Leader's Handbook*. This gave practical knowledge on how to plan ambushes and carry out sabotage. It also hinted at the savagery of guerrilla war, cautioning leaders to kill informants immediately. The third pamphlet was written by MI(R)'s explosives expert, Millis Jefferies: *How to Use High Explosives*.

These pamphlets were a start, but they did not contain much about the flip side of the agents' existence – clandestine living. The obvious place for SOE to learn this trade was from MI6, which presumably had developed sophisticated training techniques for their secret agents. Unfortunately MI6 was against providing training for SOE agents, who might be captured and reveal what they had learned. The old D Section did at least allow Gubbins to visit their training base at Brickendonbury Hall, where he no doubt came away with some useful ideas. More help came in the guise of the old *Manual of Military Intelligence in the Field*. Although firmly entrenched in the doctrine of the Great War, this document had a section on counter-espionage techniques. By reversing the instructions, from how to catch a spy to how a spy might avoid capture, the basis of the Beaulieu syllabus was developed.

The Preliminary School

Preliminary schools were envisaged as places to assess the student's character without having to reveal too much about SOE's purpose in return. Under the cover of commando training, students were put through basic military and physical training at six locations in southern England. With the constraints of secrecy, it proved difficult to teach the students anything worthwhile at these courses, and consequently three to four precious weeks were wasted waiting for their real training to begin. With country sections impatient for their students to complete the course as quickly as possible, a speedier solution was introduced. In June 1943, the preliminary course was dropped in favour of the Student's Assessment Board where candidates were put through a series of psychological and practical tests. Based at the special training school STS 7 (Winterfold House), the students were subjected to four days of tests and interviews by a panel of psychologists, psychiatrists ('trick-cyclists' in SOE slang) and military trainers, before allowing them to pass into the proper training at the Group A schools.

Paramilitary Training

Successful candidates were sent north to Scotland to undergo paramilitary training at the Group A schools.

These schools had been set up around isolated shooting lodges in the Arisaig and Morar areas of Inverness-shire. It was an area of extreme, mountainous terrain with lakes, an isolated coastline and heavy rainfall, a good place to push students to the limits of their physical and mental endurance. Based at STS 21 (Arisaig House), the students had to survive a three-week course of physical training (PT), fieldcraft, demolition, Morse code, weapons training and silent killing. The duration of the course was later increased to five weeks.

Training began with PT. There were six PT sessions a week. Students destined for clandestine work in Europe had to look like typically malnourished civilians living on paltry ration allowances, but at the same time physically become hard as nails. The PT course was therefore designed to promote fitness and endurance through running, swimming, tumbling, obstacle courses and rope work. The weather was often atrocious, but hill walking was considered an excellent means of strengthening the ankles, something that would benefit those making a parachute jump. Students were given objectives on maps and sent out on orienteering exercises day or night regardless of the conditions. Not only were they required to build up their stamina, they were expected to live off the land and learn to sleep rough under the stars or negotiate fast-moving streams of icy water. Such hard physical graft required a strong sense of camaraderie among the students and their conducting officers. Those belonging to F Section made light of the endless treks, composing their own obscene lyrics to the popular French song *Je tire ma reverence*. In their limited hours of recreation, students would poach salmon, or mount raids to steal each other's alcohol.

A still showing SOE students on a cross-country orienteering exercise. Hill walking strengthened the ankles and subconsciously prepared the agent for what might be a long walk over the Pyrenees into Spain. This was the best escape route out of occupied Europe, but the Spanish guides were notorious for not waiting on stragglers. (IWM MH24436)

Combat Training

Much of the paramilitary training programme was dedicated to weapons training, 'silent killing' and a series of knife-fighting and unarmed-combat

The rigorous training prepared SOE agents for life outdoors. Here SOE agents and partisans sleep by day after travelling by night, when there was less chance of being spotted by German reconnaissance aircraft. (IWM HU67324)

Shooting to live: students learn the Fairbairn-Sykes instinctive aiming technique. The students were taught to adopt a crouching position, draw the pistol quickly, instinctively point at the target and fire twice in quick succession without taking deliberate aim. (IWM MH24450)

techniques. The syllabus for this part of the course was the product of two remarkable officers formerly of the Shanghai Municipal Police Force. William Fairbairn and Eric Sykes were both in their late fifties when SOE came into being. They were experts in unarmed combat, pistol shooting and knife fighting. Fairbairn had studied a number of martial arts and was a ju-jitsu black belt. He shared a common interest in firearms with Sykes, who had joined the Shanghai Municipal Police sniper unit after working as a representative for Remington and Colt. In 1939 both offered their services and were recruited by MI6 D Section to teach at a secret training school at Lochailort.

The Fairbairn-Sykes approach to fighting was extremely unorthodox by regular army standards, but perfect for SOE. Based on their observations of gun crime on the Shanghai waterfront, Fairbairn and Sykes developed a method of pistol shooting that they set down in the 1942 manual *Shooting to Live*. Their experience suggested that most pistol combat occurred at distances of less than 4 yards (3.6m), with very little warning of what was about to occur. The key to survival was to be first to the draw and to get off the first shot. Even if the first shot missed, the loud report of the pistol at close range would be enough to disorientate the target temporarily and thus retain the initiative.

In contrast to the orthodox army technique of raising the pistol to eye level with the arm fully extended and then taking aim, the Fairbairn-Sykes method was to fire instinctively from hip level with a crooked arm. As part of their training regime, the student would be asked to point his forefinger quickly at

B **COMBAT TRAINING**

Using crash mats, punch-bags, straw dummies and each other, students were taught to punch, kick, use the knees and elbows, head-butt, bear-hug, chop with the side of the hand, finger jab to the eyes or the base of the throat, perform wrist holds and throws, and attack with an open-handed chin jab, among many other techniques. Improvised weapons were also used: sticks, broom handles, clipboards (for chopping), spring-loaded coshes, knuckledusters and anything that came to hand. Everything was fair game in the Fairbairn-Sykes system of fighting.

An SOE student on a realistic target range, with pop-up and mobile targets to test the reflexes and aim. Here the student is firing a Sten gun in bursts from the shoulder position for better aim. (IWM MH24447)

the object he was looking at, without raising the arm to eye level. Once the student became used to the hand-eye co-ordination, he would be taken to a firing range and asked to shoot at a target from close range. The idea of firing at a man-sized target just 2 yards (1.8m) away was to give the student confidence, and to allow the instructor to observe and correct their technique.

The student eventually worked his way up to the advanced level, by learning to shoot with one foot placed forward of the other, crouched forward as if running or stooping, this being the natural stance adopted by most people in a gunfight. The student was then expected to fire a burst of two shots in quick succession at a target no more than 3 yards (2.7m) away. A good student would be able to achieve a 'grouping' of hits at that range no wider than 6in (15cm). Once this level of speed and accuracy was achieved, the target was moved to 4 yards (3.6m), and so on.

This rapid-fire technique was another vital part of the method. Fairbairn and Sykes gave a number of anecdotes where men had been shot but had continued to fight on, or run away. They investigated if high-velocity or large-calibre ammunition had the better 'stopping power' and concluded that the effect of both was the same. In most cases they found that a bullet fired into the body was, in the short term, only as effective as the target's desire to continue fighting. Although a shot to the torso would cause a normal man to drop anything he was holding, a man charged with adrenalin might withstand a shot to the body and still shoot back. On the other hand, more success was gained by those using a Thompson submachine gun because the target was hit

Jacqueline Nearne approaches a mocked-up house on the SOE range. As the target appears in the doorway, the agent crouches forward and fires. The targets were controlled by levers operated by a technician overlooking the course from a cliff top. (IWM MH24441)

repeatedly in quick succession. To replicate this effect with a pistol, Fairbairn and Sykes argued that the best way to stop a determined target was to hit it twice. This method is now called the 'double tap'.

When the students were completely confident in pistol shooting, they were sent out on a type of assault course at the foot of a cliff. Above them was an instructor armed with a series of levers. As the students walked their way through the course, the instructor would cause targets to spring up in their path. There were other devices that sent the target flying toward the students, and others like a fairground shooting gallery, where the target passed from side to side.

In addition to pistols, SOE students were shown how to fire and maintain all the standard Allied light weapons. They were also allowed to practise on captured German weapons like MP38s and MP40s, Lugers, Mauser rifles and a variety of machine guns. The most common SOE weapon was the Sten submachine gun. This easily concealed, robust weapon was sent to resistance networks by the thousand. It used European 9mm ammunition and could be fired in single shots or bursts. It was visually distinguished by the magazine that protruded from the left-hand side. Students were taught that holding the magazine during firing could cause a misfire, so they should grip the gun underneath by the cooling cylinder instead. For best results, they were taught to fire the Sten from the shoulder in single shots in order to retain control of the weapon. In that regard the Sten was superior to the Thompson because it weighed 3lb (1.4kg) less.

The Sten Mark II submachine gun, as modelled by this tribal chieftain in northern Albania. The Sten was the perfect weapon for guerrilla warfare and was supplied by the thousand by SOE. It was cheap to produce, easy to fire, could use captured German ammunition and was capable of being broken down and hidden in a shopping bag. (IWM HU64787)

Silent Killing

The Fairbairn-Sykes training method is best remembered for its use of the knife and martial arts. Fairbairn developed a style of fighting based on some of the techniques of judo and Chinese boxing, but concentrating on 'dirty' tactics of targeting the opponent's eyes and testicles. This 'all-in fighting' was brutal, and one might wonder if many students were too squeamish to contemplate actually using the techniques. The way in which the training was delivered made the students think aggressively, and taught them to react without pause. An example of how effective this method was can be found with SOE agent Nancy Wake. While sneaking up on a target, a German sentry turned and faced her. Without thinking, she instinctively attacked the bigger man and broke his neck with a swift open-handed blow.

Students were shown how to turn parry into attack. Working on the theory that action is always faster than reaction, students were taught to spin round if an enemy held a pistol into their back. They were shown how to tackle opponents armed with a bayonet and rifle, seizing the muzzle of the rifle in one hand, pushing it to one side, while pirouetting in the opposite direction and

Agent Profile – Pearl Witherington

Born in 1914 to British parents in Paris, Pearl Witherington worked as a secretary to the Air Attaché at the British Embassy before the German invasion. She escaped France with the help of the resistance and reached England in July 1941. Working at the Air Ministry, Pearl pushed for a more active role and so was transferred to SOE.

Her training began on 8 June 1943. The instructor's remarks show that Pearl was a determined student, noting under weapons training: 'Probably the best shot (male or female) we have yet had.' They were equally pleased with her demolition work: 'Extremely keen on this and would like to specialize.' Summing up the instructor recorded: 'This student, though a woman, has definitely got leaders' qualities.' The training commandant concurred: 'An excellent student for the job. Knows what she is in for and is anxious to get on with it.'

Pearl's only weakness was Morse code. Unsuitable as a radio operator, she was chosen as a courier to work with the STATIONER circuit under 'Hector', the codename of SOE officer Maurice Southgate. Pearl was parachuted into France on the night of 22 September 1943. Having promised her mother not to return to France, Pearl pretended that she had been posted to North Africa. In her absence, SOE wrote letters to her mother each month enclosing money from Pearl's £350-a-year wages.

To avoid detection while delivering messages for Hector, Pearl travelled by night, or first class by train. Instructed to make contact with Colonel Villiers, a Frenchman believed to command a large Maquis, she gained his support in sabotaging the Michelin tyre works at Clermont-Ferrand. Unfortunately Villiers' top saboteur was arrested while planting incendiaries in a workshop, the scheme failed and the plant continued to turn out material for the Germans.

Following SOE's success in having Peugeot sabotage its own factory (see p51), Pearl made a similar offer to Michelin's management. Michelin initially agreed to the proposal, but then refused to co-operate, believing that the RAF was too busy with invasion preparations to bomb Clermont-Ferrand. They were badly mistaken. Reporting only light anti-aircraft defences around the plant, Pearl sent a message to London: 'I hate to suggest this bombing of Michelin but Villiers and I think it would give the management a lesson.' On 5 April 1944, she was able to report that the plant had been completely destroyed.

Villiers was arrested by the Gestapo in Montluçon on 1 May and sent to Buchenwald. The STATIONER territory was broken into smaller areas, with Pearl promoted as organizer for the new WRESTLER circuit in the Cher valley. At the head of several thousand Maquis, Pearl successfully disrupted the movement of German reinforcements and supplies to the Allied bridgehead in Normandy. With a 1,000,000 Francs bounty on her head, she survived several close scrapes with German troops.

Fate threw her together with resister Henri Cornioley, her pre-war fiancé. After the liberation of France, they came to London and married on 26 October 1944. For taking command of a circuit, Pearl was recommended for the Military Cross. Unfortunately, as a civilian she was considered ineligible for the award and was offered an MBE instead. She refused this civilian award, claiming she had done nothing 'civil' to deserve it. She was also denied her parachute wings having only completed four drops, rather than the necessary five. This was because female agents only had to make three training jumps, one less than the men, who gained their wings making the fifth, operational jump. In 2006 the Parachute Regiment relented and awarded her parachute wings.

From Marie.   11.3.44.

Michelin.

1) I regret to inform you that the proposed sabotage of Michelin has completely fallen thro' in spite of repeated attacks. The management, after agreeing to the proposed destruction, refused to collaborate and still do so. Villiers' sabotage leader has been arrested: he tried to set fire to the M. factory by putting thirty incendiaries in one workshop, he did not take into consideration the working of the "dispositif de securité d'incendie".

2) I wish to put on record the management's attitude vis à vis the sabotage plans. They refuse to believe the R.A.F. will have time to bomb Clermont-Ferrand before an allied landing: in the meantime they are working, turning out material and making money whereas if the sabotage had taken place when proposed they would be doing none of these today.

They are playing for time.

3) If it is decided to destroy Michelin by bombing the factory, the R.A.F. could also bomb Bergougnan where they are turning out material exclusively for the Huns.

4) There is very little defence around Clermont-Ferrand and what there is, is mobile.

5) I hate to suggest the bombing of M. but Villiers and I think it would give the management a lesson and force Villiers' hand if Clermont-Ferrand were bombed.

Marie.

5/4/44.

Michelin was well pin pointed and destruction complete in main factory. People in Clermont say many of the incendiaries were duds. Casualties about 16 killed & 20 injured. Sanatorium damaged by blast, no casualties or damaged material.

Re my para 3 above, Hector is dealing.

Marie.

From MARIE   22.3.44.

Distribution :
1 - D/R
1 - MG/TGT Pour DR/IN5
1 - F Sec Circ
1 - Marie file   Brought back by Lysander 9/10th April 44.

MICHELIN

1.   I regret to inform you that the proposed sabotage of MICHELIN has completely fallen thro' in spite of repeated attacks. The management, after agreeing to the proposed destruction, refused to collaborate and still do so. Villiers' sabotage leader has been arrested: he tried to set fire to the MICHELIN factory by putting thirty incendiaries in one workshop; he did not take into consideration the working of the 'dispositif de sécurité d'incendie'.

2.   I wish to put on record the management's attitude vis-à-vis the sabotage plans. They refuse to believe the R.A.F. will have time to bomb Clermont Ferrand before an allied landing: in the meantime they are working turning out material and making money whereas, if the sabotage had taken place when proposed they would be doing none of these to-day. They are playing for time.

3.   If it is decided to destroy MICHELIN by bombing the factory, the R.A.F. could also bomb BERGOUGNAN where they are turning out material exclusively for the Huns.

4.   There is very little defence around Clermont Ferrand and what there is is mobile.

5.   I hate to suggest this bombing of MICHELIN but Villiers and I think it would give the management a lesson and force Villiers' hand if Clermont Ferrand were bombed.

(signed) MARIE.

..../.

5.4.44.

MICHELIN was well pin-pointed and destruction complete in main factory. People in Clermont say many of the incendiaries were duds. Casualties: about 16 killed and 20 injured. Sanatorium damaged by blast, no casualties or damaged material.

Re my para 3 above, HECTOR is dealing.

(signed) MARIE.

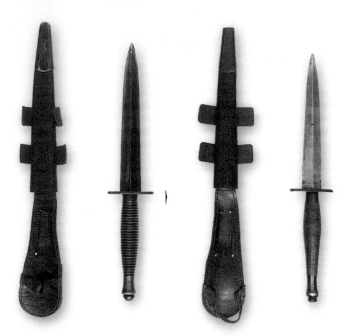

elbowing them in the face. They were taught never to go to ground in a fight, but to always get up in case an unseen opponent dealt them a blow to the back of the head. They were also taught never to fight a crowd of opponents, but to keep moving and to escape as quickly as possible.

Fairbairn and Sykes both had a healthy respect for knife fighters, and claimed that unless the student had a firearm, the only defence against a skilled opponent holding a knife was to run as fast as possible. The pair had developed the FS commando knife. This featured a double-edged blade, so designed to prevent the opponent gripping the blade. Because even a wooden replica would be too dangerous to practise with, students were given lengths of rope and practised delivering hits on the 22 points where a lethal wound could be made on the human body.

Examples of the Fairbairn-Sykes fighting knife issued to SOE agents from 1941 onwards. First designed in 1933, the knife was designed to be used for slashing and thrusting. With an overall length of 11½in (29.2cm), the blade had a length of 6¼in (15.9cm). This blade was considered long enough to penetrate the overcoat and uniform of even the thickest cloth. (IWM MH13087)

Students were taught to ignore the rules of war and never take prisoners unless that was their specific intention. There was a particularly efficient means of searching prisoners. The students were told to make the prisoner lay down with his arms outstretched and then kill him, or knock him unconscious if there was some very good reason why killing him would be inconvenient. The search would then prove much easier to undertake. It was a brutal world the students had entered.

Demolition Training

Demolition training was an essential part of the Group A syllabus. Railway sabotage was particularly important to SOE and it was imperative that all

Film still showing Harry Ree (left) and Jacqueline Nearne (centre) being instructed in rail sabotage. Nearne is taping plastic explosive (PE) under the rail while Ree places a fog signal detonator on top. Several lengths of track were set up for SOE to destroy as part of the Group A paramilitary school. (IWM MH24449)

students had some practical experience in using explosives. Using dummy bombs, rail sabotage was carried out with the cooperation of the West Highland Line, which also supplied the school with a train. Students were taught how to lay their charges and then make their getaway. There was much for trainee saboteurs to learn. SOE had access to a wide range of military and commercial explosives like gelignite and amatol. Students were also given recipes for homemade bombs made out of commercially available weedkiller and fertilizers. By preference, the explosive of choice was the recently developed Nobel 808 Plastic Explosive (PE), a safe, malleable explosive that could be dyed and shaped as required. The beauty of PE, other than the ease with which it could be disguised, was its stability. It could be tossed around and was even safe if hit by a bullet.

Explosives require a fuse to allow the user time to get clear and, in the case of PE, a primer to set off the main charge. The primer had to deliver either an electric spark or a small explosion. An electric charge could be administered by the use of an 'exploder', the classic box and plunger type of device. The advantage of such a system was that the operator could decide the exact moment at which detonation occurred, particularly useful if the target was a moving vehicle. The downside was that the operator had to be close by and ran the risk of being caught.

Such risks led to the creation of the 'Time Pencil', or more properly, the Switch No. 10. Originally developed by the Germans during World War I, the Time Pencil came to Britain by way of Poland in 1939. The device was a thin brass or aluminium tube 5in (12.7cm) long containing a spring-loaded striker and safety fuse. One section of the pencil was made of copper and contained a glass ampoule containing copper chloride. To operate the device, the saboteur squeezed the copper tube, crushing the ampoule and releasing the fluid, which dissolved a steel wire to release the striker and detonate the fuse. There were five types of Time Pencil, each colour-coded to indicate different delay periods: black (10 minutes); red (30 minutes); green (5½ hours); yellow (12 hours); and blue (24 hours). Normal operation was affected by variations

The 'Demonstration Room' at STN XVb, better known as London's Natural History Museum. The room was commandeered by SOE, and a host of booby traps, secret devices and clandestine equipment was put on show for visiting dignities, including King George VI. (IWM HU61060)

in temperature and Time Pencils took significantly longer to function in extreme cold. The black and red varieties were also prone to go off early and were distrusted by many agents for that reason.

An alternative means of detonation was to leave booby traps with instantaneous switches triggered by the application or release of pressure, or by a pull-switch attached to a trip wire. A widely used example of a pressure device was the explosive tyre-burster. This was a small cylinder 2in × ¾in (5cm × 1.9cm) containing PE and was activated when 150lb (68kg) of pressure was applied. They were often hidden in animal dung or disguised as pebbles.

On railways a modified 'fog signal' was used to activate an explosive charge. The fog signal was a device used to warn locomotive drivers of red signals ahead in foggy conditions. The device was secured to the track, and as the front wheel of the train passed over it the fog signal would detonate, emitting a sharp, audible bang. The SOE device worked on the same principles, but it was linked to an explosive charge through fuse cord. The drawback with this device was its visibility. If the Germans patrolled the tracks, they would easily spot the fog signals, a fact that led some agents to add a crude anti-tamper device consisting of a hand grenade, with the safety pin removed, strapped to the underside of the device: if the sentry picked up the main device, the grenade would explode.

Another detonation method was to use concealed pressure switches. The saboteur would remove ballast from under a rail, insert a charge and then place a pressure switch set against the underside of the rail. The ballast was then replaced, making the device difficult to detect by patrols. As the train passed over the rail, the weight of the locomotive's wheels would depress the rail and activate the charge. As the Germans became wise to these devices, they often ran a locomotive ahead of trains with important cargoes, detonating any explosive devices placed on the line with an expendable vehicle. To get round this, SOE developed the 'Imber Switch' – a pressure switch that would allow the first train to go over, and then detonate when the next train passed. Students also had to learn how to use limpet mines and 'clams', which allowed an explosive device to be attached to metallic objects magnetically. The explosive charge was contained in a box, and the magnets on six adjustable legs (three on each side) protruded from the main charge. All the user had to do was attach the legs to the target and insert a fuse as usual.

 PARACHUTE TRAINING

The final part of the Group A syllabus was parachute training at RAF Ringway, near Manchester. The first sessions saw the students perform landing practice from harnesses onto crash mats. Here they learnt to perfect the technique of keeping the legs together to prevent breaks, and to perform a roll to soften the impact from landing. Once these basic techniques were mastered, the students were taken for their first practice jump. This was not from an aircraft, but from a tethered barrage balloon. The students and instructor would be suspended in a box-like cage with a large central trap door, 700ft (213m) up in the air. At the word of command, the student had to throw himself off and hope for the best. Many found jumping from a static balloon unnerving compared to jumping from a speeding aircraft. Despite having been through everything the wilds of Scotland had to offer, for some this jump was too much and they were failed. Others quietly asked their instructors to give them a push if they appeared to freeze. Afterwards, the students were required to perform at least two jumps from aircraft before earning their parachute wings.

FINISHING SCHOOL AND FIELD SKILLS

At the end of the Group A course, each student had to negotiate a series of natural and manmade obstacles. At various stages through the course, they were required to fire at targets using all the weapons in which they had been trained. This was followed by a gruelling 24-hour, long-distant trek through the mountains. For those that passed this feat of endurance, there was one final test of courage. Students were sent for parachute training at RAF Ringway, near Manchester (see Plate C).

Next stop on the itinerary were the Group B finishing schools at Beaulieu in the New Forest. These were designed to prepare the students for the intricacies of clandestine living. Eighty students could be accommodated in 11 houses on the estate. Each day would begin with two hours of PT and unarmed combat to keep the students sharp, but otherwise the syllabus was more mentally than physically demanding. The three-week course was divided into five classes: Department A taught the techniques of clandestine living; Department B a series of practical exercises to test knowledge of these techniques; Department C taught enemy organization; Department D propaganda; and Department E codes. Once Beaulieu had been successfully negotiated, the students were sent back to their respective country sections where their missions would at last be explained and they would be given a cover story to explain their sudden appearance.

Clandestine Living

There was much to impart on how to live behind enemy lines. Having arrived in occupied territory, agents were cautioned to take things slowly at first. For accommodation they were advised to go to modest-sized hotels where they would be fairly anonymous. They were cautioned against small guest houses, hostels and lodgings where there would be more chance of arousing suspicion. It was believed that the best solution for a male agent was to find a girlfriend living in a villa in a remote area. They were cautioned against basing themselves in a brothel, as prostitutes were routinely used as police informers in Europe.

Over the first few days, the agent was to get the feel for the place and begin building up his cover story. Things that might catch an agent out were questions like 'where did you have your last haircut' or 'where did you have your laundry done?' He was also to get the measure of the local police and find the location of garrisons. The agent might be unlucky enough to land at a time when the Germans were tearing the countryside apart looking for an Allied airman or escapee. Without taking the opportunity to learn these basic things, the agent's life was in grave danger.

After this the agent would have to locate safe houses where he could go for a meal and a night's sleep. Agents were cautioned against remaining too long at the same safe house and many agents would move on every night. The agent would always arrange some system so the landlords could warn them not to knock on the door if it was dangerous – one example being an empty birdcage being placed in the window. Of all the safe houses found by SOE agents, the least predictable was found by radio operator Denis Rake, who worked as a transvestite singer in a Parisian club and lived with a like-minded German officer in Paris for five months. Such arrangements must be considered exceptional in the extreme.

A great amount of information was given in the recruitment of sub-agents, in assigning them roles within the organization and, above all, maintaining security. It was highly likely that enemy security organizations would try to infiltrate stool pigeons into resistance groups. It was therefore important to organize sub-agents into cells that were unaware of each other's existence. If one cell was captured or betrayed, the other groups would have a better chance of remaining anonymous. Even if the leader was picked up, he would only know the leaders of each cell, not the individual members, or the location of their hideouts.

A successful means of communication had to be found to keep all the groups in touch. Telephone communication was subject to interception so was out of the question. Face-to-face meetings were also extremely hazardous. Agents were told to ignore one another in the street unless they had specifically arranged to meet. It was better to pass coded messages through third parties, or 'cut-outs' or 'letter boxes' (e.g. the owners of tobacconists, or newspaper kiosks), or 'dead letter boxes' (a hiding place, for example under a particular stone). The best method was to use a relay of couriers so that none of them knew the whole route the message would have to pass through, or from where it had come. Although many couriers knew what they were doing, it was possible to use 'dead couriers' – people who had no idea they were carrying messages for a resistance network.

Agents might also be called upon to gather intelligence before conducting a mission. For this they might have to break into an office or factory and steal important blueprints. SOE students were taught a wide range of criminal skills at Beaulieu by a number of colourful experts. The first instructor of this course was the Glaswegian safebreaker Johnny Ramensky. A one-man crime wave, Ramensky had spent most of his adult life in prison and for one escape bid received the dubious honour of being the last person in Scottish penal history to be shackled to the wall of his prison cell. Undoubtedly a master of his art, the authorities gave Ramensky the chance to do his bit for the war effort by teaching SOE agents his skills. Ramensky's *pièce de résistance* was the art of blowing up safes without damaging the contents or bringing down the walls and ceiling. After his stint with SOE, Ramensky went on commando missions himself and is believed to have been one of the first

Allied troops into Rome in 1944 where, it is rumoured, he blew the safes of 14 embassies in a single day. A hard act to follow, Ramensky was replaced by 'Killer' Green. Long believed to be an ex-con like Ramensky, Green was in fact a former accountant turned captain in the Intelligence Corps.

The criminal syllabus included advice on stakeouts, forced entry, slipping locks and breaking windows silently. Students were shown how to make casts of keys in a bar of soap or plasticine and to cut a key from the lid of a tobacco tin. They were taught how to slip out of handcuffs and perform simple forgery techniques. As part of the course, students would have to break into buildings on the estate. Negotiating their way across gravely paths and hidden trip wires, they would shimmy up drains and prise open upper-storey windows to steal an agreed objective. The traps set to expose the students in these exercises were quite often set by Captain 'Nobby' Clarke, a gamekeeper from the Royal Estate at Sandringham. When not trying to catch students, Clarke taught poaching skills like setting snares, stalking and how to live off the land.

With the lessons explained in the classroom environment, it was time to test the students' practical application. They were sent into local cities like Bournemouth, and given some scheme to enact. This might be something as simple as shadowing a person and seeing where they went or making contact with a 'cut-out' at some preordained location. It might also be to ensure that no one was following them. The students were taught to stand and look into shop windows to watch the reflection of people standing behind them. A good way of shaking a tail was to get onto a bus, tram or train, and then jump off at the last second. Another way was to go into a busy department store and lose them. What the students did not know was that they were being stalked by police and Special Branch officers. Each agent carried a letter on them – a get out of jail free card – to be produced if they were caught by the authorities. The best students maintained their charade even after capture and tried to bluff their way out of arrest. Much more was thought of these individuals than those who revealed their secret vocation at the first enquiry.

Following the maxim of 'know your enemy', students were taught about the internal functions of the German police state. The various roles of Gestapo, Sipo, Kripo, SD, SS, Abwehr, Feldgendarmerie were all explained, along with 'puppet' organizations like the French Milice. Agents and resisters returning from the field kept this information up to date, and explained the various interrogation methods used on captives. Although brutality was to be expected, agents were filled with information useful to the enemy, who would prefer to keep them alive, albeit temporarily, long enough to extract it. Students were told to expect treatment designed to humiliate and depress them. To reinforce this message, students would be hauled out of bed in the middle of the night by SOE staff dressed in Nazi uniforms and be subjected to terrifying mock interrogations.

The point of these interrogations was to reinforce the notion of holding out for 48 hours and give enough time for the rest of the organization to scatter. Of course the Germans knew the agent would try to hold out this long and so would go all-out to make the agent speak as quickly as possible. One torture-resistance technique taught was to attempt slow counting in one's head, trying to ignore everything else that was going on. It was not unknown for captives to offer their interrogators bribes, posing as black-market profiteers. In most cases, agents knew they were in for a hiding if captured, and naturally enough this subject was not dwelt upon too much by the trainers.

There was another way of tripping students up. Girls working for SOE were set up to play the part of 'honeytraps' against male students. Towards the end of the course an instructor would take a male student into town and buy him a drink at a hotel. In the lobby the instructor would happen to see one of the girls on the staff and call her over. After an invite to make up a threesome for dinner, the instructor would be called away to take a telephone call and then announce he had to leave. The student would be left to have dinner with the girl on his own, during which time the girl would probe the agent for information on what he was doing to help win the war. Occasionally a combination of vanity and loneliness got the better of the fellow and he confessed in hushed tones that he was a secret agent about to be parachuted into enemy territory where almost certain death awaited. The dinner companion would feign surprise and admiration, then report the man's indiscretions to his instructor next morning. Despite weeks of intensive training, that would be the end of his career.

The next phase of the training at Beaulieu was somewhat more lofty, but equally important. Propaganda lessons were first put together by Kim Philby, who was uniquely qualified to teach lessons on the clandestine arts. Unknown to his colleagues at the time, Philby was a Soviet spy. His course centred on promoting the idea of resistance to the various peoples of the occupied countries and was vital if the student was going to galvanize support.

Not everyone in occupied Europe was prepared to join resistance cells as active members, or hide weapons and so on, but more were prepared to cooperate passively – to turn a blind eye or perhaps make the odd pinprick against the Third Reich, if nothing could be traced back to them. The role of propaganda was to turn neutrals into passive resisters and encourage passive resisters to become active ones. During World War II the BBC had a policy of broadcasting news as accurately as possible and built up a reputation that would have been shattered if it started telling obvious lies. Black propaganda was the

Scene from a Group B lesson. Students are taught how to organize resistance cells, while uniform identification charts on the walls at the back of the class show all known German rank markings. (IWM MH24437)

preserve of the PWE. This was the organization that faked German radio shows and newspapers and dropped propaganda leaflets on German cities. Such propaganda could only be targeted at wide groups (all civilians or all soldiers), while an SOE agent on the ground could actually target specific groups, for instance farmers forced to hand over their produce to the German Army.

The Philby lecture explained to students how to convince groups they *should* and *could* take action, appealing to their self-interest as much as their patriotism. One of the key messages was that everyone could play their part. You did not need to wield a gun to damage the German war machine. Through small random acts of sabotage, recalcitrance or even overzealous attention to detail, factory and railway workers could help bring the Nazi war economy to a grinding halt. The possibilities were endless: filling out forms incorrectly, referencing letters wrongly, misfiling index cards, giving wrong telephone numbers, answering questions with drawn-out explanations – using 20 words where a single word would do. Lorry drivers could drive slowly to create traffic jams, drive in the lowest gear and insert sharp stones in the tyres. Porters could drop boxes marked 'fragile' destined for laboratories. They could stack goods compartments in such a way that the boxes fell over when a train moved, or chalk the wrong number on the side of wagons. Guards on trains could lock lavatory doors in the 'engaged' position when German VIPs were onboard. Postmen could deliver mail to the wrong addresses. Electricians could smash light bulbs while carrying ladders, or accidentally overload power circuits and cause cut-outs. Scientists could design minute flaws into blueprints, and welders might under-heat rivets. Anyone could denounce a Quisling as 'unreliable', or make false reports of guerrilla activity and so on. Everyone could resist in some way. It was the agent's job to promote this.

Secret Communications

The final part of the Beaulieu course was dedicated to secret communications and code work. It was mentally draining and one of the most difficult aspects of the course. Cipher work was more suited to crossword addicts than men of action and many struggled to understand the complex process of using a simple poem to convert a message into a seemingly unintelligible scramble of letters. SOE started out using a system known as Playfair, used extensively in the 1914–18 war and named after Sir Lyon Playfair, the Victorian scientist who championed the system. The agent was asked to remember a short poem,

MOCK INTERROGATION

When SOE agents were near the end of their training at Beaulieu, some of the trainers would dress up as Nazis and pull a student out of bed in the middle of the night, yelling at him, then begin a quite fierce interrogation. This part of the course was dreaded by most students, but was a useful ordeal to go through. Escapees reported that the German technique was to make agents feel embarrassed or ridiculous during an interrogation in order to break them mentally. If captured in civilian dress, there was no point trying to give name, rank and number. The agents would have to remember the entire personal life history from their cover stories. Even then, if they claimed they were from such-and-such a village, there was always the chance the interrogator would order an enquiry to take place. The other important element was to have a second cover story ready if the first story unravelled – for instance, that they were shot-down Allied pilots trying to get home. The authorities might be more willing to believe the second story and, if nothing else, it would buy more time for others to escape while the facts were checked. The agents had it drummed into them that they had to hold out for 48 hours to give everyone a chance to escape.

An SOE officer consults his code book while on operations with partisans in Yugoslavia. (IWM HU57246)

or verse. In desperation an agent might use the Lord's Prayer, but it could be any verse at all, provided it had been agreed with the recipient in advance. The agent would then select five words at random from the verse, and provide an indicator at the beginning of the message so the recipient would know which five words had been chosen. In this case we will select 'Our– Father – heaven – be – thy.' A 5 × 5 grid would then be drawn up and the letters of the key group inserted in order, using each letter only once:

O	U	R	F	A
T	H	E	V	N
B	Y			

Once all the letters in the verse were used up, the remainder of the alphabet was inserted into the square in correct sequential order (C/D/G/K/L/M/P/Q/S/V/X/Z). To reduce the alphabet to 25 letters 'I' and 'J' would be combined:

O	U	R	F	A
T	H	E	V	N
B	Y	C	D	G
I/J	K	L	M	P
Q	S	W	X	Z

If the agent wished to encipher the word 'parachute' he would first write the word into two-letter groups: PA RA CH UT EX – the letter 'X' being added to make the last single letter into a pair. The agent would circle the letters P and A on the grid and then find the diagonal reflection of the group to covert PA to IO:

O	U	R	F	A
T	H	E	V	N
B	Y	C	D	G
I/J	K	L	M	P
Q	S	W	X	Z

Continuing on with this method, the next route of letters would be *RA*. Because 'R' and 'A' were on the same line as each other on the grid and do not form a diagonal, the letters shift one place along the grid to the right giving FO. Notice that when the last letter of the line is reached (in this case 'A'), it returns to the beginning of the line. Likewise if the letters had appeared on the same column (e.g. LW) each letter is shifted down one place, giving WR. Continuing with the cipher, the next group (CH) forms a diagonal with YE; UT with OH; and EX with VW. Thus parachute becomes IO-FO-YE-OH-VW.

Ingenious as this may seem, the cipher had its disadvantages. The biggest was that messages under 200 words long were relatively simple to break. This was particularly true if a word had any double letters in it, for example *moon* or *attack*. The enemy codebreaker would look for repetitions like this and, knowing there were only a limited number of possible letters you could write doubles with, would quickly make his first break. To get round this agents were told to insert a dud letter between the two letters, thus *attack* would become *atxtack*. To muddle things further, rather than using Shakespeare or even the National Anthem, the agents were encouraged to come up with their own poems, or rhyming ditties, many of which were outrageously smutty.

More secure, but still not ideal, was the method known as 'double transposition'. The agent in the field would either use a poem to provide the key words or select them from a specialist chosen book, of which the recipient had the same edition. The agent would select two words in the book, each 8–20 characters long, and give the recipient the page number, the line each word was taken from, and how many words along that line it appeared. Thus only the two owners of that book would know the keywords.

Using the key words SEAHORSE and MINOTAUR, our agent is going to send London the following message: 'Factory destroyed. Call off RAF.' The first stage was to write out a grid with SEAHORSE along the top, with a numerical value added to each letter beginning with the first 'A'. If a letter appeared more than once in the word, the one to the left would receive precedence:

S	E	A	H	O	R	S	E
7	2	1	4	5	6	8	3

The message would now be written into the columns below the keyword. If punctuation marks were required STOP and COMMA were written in full. Unlike the Playfair system, it was important that the last row of the column was incomplete, even if it meant inserting dud letters to achieve this:

S	E	A	H	O	R	S	E
7	2	1	4	5	6	8	3
F	A	C	T	O	R	Y	D
E	S	T	R	O	Y	E	D
S	T	O	P	C	A	L	L
O	F	F	R	A	F		

Having filled in the grid, the agent would now draw up a second table with the second key word, and assign each letter a numerical value as before:

M	I	N	O	T	A	U	R
S	2	4	5	7	1	8	6

The agent would then copy from the first table the letters in column one, and write them vertically onto the second grid as follows:

M	I	N	O	T	A	U	R
S	2	4	5	7	1	8	6
C	T	O	F				

The process would continue, copying the columns in numerical sequence as follows:

M	I	N	O	T	A	U	R
S	2	4	5	7	1	8	6
C	T	O	F	A	S	T	F
D	D	L	T	R	P	R	O
O	C	A	R	Y	A	F	F
E	S	O	Y	E	L		

Reading the columns on the second grid in sequential order, the agent would now copy out the ciphered key as follows: SPAL TDCS CDOE OLAO FOF ARYE TRF. For transmitting, the sequence would be arranged into groups of five letters, the final version of the message reading: SPALT DCSCD OEOLA OFOFA RYETR F.

Again, this seemingly complex procedure had its faults. In effect, the process did nothing but render the message into a complex anagram puzzle. To increase security, agents were advised to write longer messages, but no more than 200 using the same key words. It might be necessary with longer messages to transmit them separately, using a different code word for each.

Although he would swear blind to the agents that double transposition codes were the most secure available, the man in charge of SOE's agent codes knew they were highly susceptible to German cryptographers. Leo Marks developed a new system for SOE called the Worked Out Key (WOK) system, better known as the 'one-time pad'. Marks had identified that the agent's codes were flawed because once the Germans worked out the key, they could intercept future messages at will. The one-time pad was a piece of silk with a series of transposition keys pre-printed. The agent would have one copy of it; home base the other. Once the key was used, the agent destroyed it and moved on to the next key printed alongside it. The central advantage of this system was that if the agent was captured, he would not be able to remember the discarded keys previously used. Marks' excellent autobiography *Between Silk and Cyanide* explains how this system was developed and how it was only finally introduced in 1943, despite the obvious weaknesses of its predecessors.

As last resort, agents had a number of means to communicate with home. Even in wartime, all the foreign press found its way to England through neutral countries within a week. Agents were told to insert a coded message into an advertisement, or under the 'articles lost' section. The only drawback with this technique is that it was a well-known trick of the spy trade and all such messages were carefully scrutinized by enemy counter-intelligence.

There was perhaps more chance of getting a message out through a seemingly innocent letter via cover addresses in a neutral country like Switzerland. There were rules to this procedure, however. As letters were subject to tight censorship, a means would have to be used to disguise the secret message. It was therefore very unlikely that an anonymous letter addressed to the British consulate in a neutral country would get through with the Playfair message: LFWYF UXCDK UPHWV WWLMW WCTHF UUZVB PTZVC EWZ

The most obvious way of concealing a message was to use secret ink, which could be made in the field by any number of means. Unfortunately, both sides of the conflict had developed sophisticated ways of detecting this sort of writing. A simpler way was to disguise a message in a seemingly innocent piece of text, for example:

This year spring came quite early. With the nice weather I decided against any new plans until Easter has passed. When will you receive news of Aunt Rachel's son, David? Is he in the services or did he stick with his education until all this finishes?

If you circle every third word of the message you have the following groups of words.

Spring Early Nice Decided New Easter When
Receive Aunt David In Or Stick Education This

By reading the first letter of each word, you can extract the message: SEND NEW RADIO SET.

Of course, in a real situation a successful agent would have first enciphered the message. Without knowing what the gap between the coded words was (in this case it was every third word), and without knowing the key to the cipher, it really was almost impossible to break this system. For that reason it was extensively used between resistance groups in the field.

There was another means for agents to communicate with their commanders: the S-Phone. Capable of being packed into a suitcase, it was a microwave wireless set that allowed a person on the ground to have the equivalent of a telephone conversation with a person in an aircraft or boat, and with reasonable security. The best use of this device was not for navigation but for SOE agents to hold crisis meetings with staff officers, who could fly out and pass instructions. From the point of view of London, if there was any suspicion that the Germans had taken over a network, the S-Phone allowed them to speak to the agent and confirm his safety through voice recognition.

Without secure communications to one of the SOE's Home Stations dotted around the globe, little could be accomplished by an agent. An underground movement

A radio operator has set up his B2 suitcase wireless on a makeshift desk of jerry cans. Wearing headphones, he appears to be taking down a coded message in Morse code. (IWM HU64885)

First in a series of stills showing how to set up the perfect site for receiving parachute drops. The first stage after locating a large enough field was to test wind direction. Note the boxes containing the Eureka transmitting device. (IWM MH24446)

needed weapons and equipment, so one of the key tasks of an SOE agent was to organize supply. This normally meant having an aircraft drop parachute containers at a prearranged site. The agent would send a message to their Home Station, suggesting a convenient site well away from prying eyes. Great detail was required in organizing reception committees for supply drops. Large fields would have to be found in discreet locations away from German garrisons or local police headquarters. Transport was needed to remove the containers to hiding places, which would have to be prepared in advance.

Once a request made for a supply drop was confirmed the agent would receive a radio message, or, as was the case in France, the BBC would broadcast a 'personal message' out to the agent on the evening news confirming that the drop would go ahead. The vast majority of supply drops occurred at night, which meant the RAF (and later USAAF) would need some way of identifying they were in the right place. The aircrew relied on people at the drop zone giving them a signal. As blazing fires would be seen for miles around, the agent would arrange three men at 100m (109-yard) intervals in a line, each armed with electric flashlights. A fourth man would stand to one side of the line, giving it an inverted 'L' shape. He would flash a prearranged letter in Morse code on his flashlight. The aircrew would spot the line and then confirm the correct recognition signal was being used before dropping the cargo.

Learning the signal procedure for parachute drops. The welcoming committee would form an inverted 'L' shape in the field and hold flashlights toward the sky. One agent would use a flashlight to send an agreed recognition letter in Morse code. Without that signal, the aircrew were told to abort and return home, lest Germans had overrun the landing site. (IWM MH24443)

In addition to arranging supply drops, students were also taught how to prepare emergency landing strips for aircraft like the Westland Lysander or the Lockheed Hudson light bomber. Both types of aircraft were used to infiltrate and exfiltrate agents or other important personages from behind enemy lines. Landing in a field at night was a risky business, so the welcoming committee would need to ensure a relatively flat surface, with no trees and all fences and other impedimenta removed in

advance (and replaced by morning so no one became suspicious). The Lysander required 400m (437 yards) in which to land and take off, while the Hudson required a clearing 1km (0.6 mile) in length.

Supply drops and pick-ups theoretically became more accurate with the introduction of the Eureka/Rebecca device. The Eureka half of the system was a ground beacon transmitting a pulse that was recognized by the Rebecca device in the aircraft. This system allowed the aircrew navigator to pick up the signal at least 20 miles (32 km) away and could guide them in to within 200m (219 yards) of the drop zone. The downside to the system was it was heavy to carry and too complex for many untrained resisters to understand. The system was so poorly employed that from September 1943 SOE felt it necessary to set up a 10-day Eureka/Rebecca course at STS 40 (Howbury Hall).

The Eureka transmitter is set up ready to transmit a signal that the supply aircraft could home in on from at least 20 miles (32km) away. Although a brilliant means of guiding aircraft to within 200m (219 yards) of the landing site, it is obvious from this image how bulky the Eureka was to carry around and hide. (IWM MH24442)

Industrial Sabotage

With the general syllabus covered, students were free to return to their country sections and become fully fledged agents in the field. Before this occurred many of them required additional specialist training courses to help them fulfil their missions. One of the best-attended of these was the three-week industrial sabotage course at STS 17 (Brickendonbury Manor) taught by Lieutenant-Colonel George Rheam. Having already received basic training in explosives during the paramilitary school phase, Rheam's course was designed to perfect the art of crippling the Nazi war economy.

Through the different phases of the war, sabotage had distinct priorities. During the early stages of the conflict, the first targets were German petroleum stocks. As the war moved into the skies and seas around Britain, aircraft and then U-boat production facilities were targeted. As the situation stabilized, target

Industrial sabotage school. A Royal Engineers officer demonstrates the weak points of steam locomotives on the underside of a scale model steam engine. With some parts harder to replace than others, SOE students were taught to target the cylinder with explosives, as repairs would take months to complete. (IWM MH24439)

Some of the best targets for industrial sabotage were those responsible for electric power supply. Here students are shown the best way to sabotage electricity transformers: these were far harder to replace than downed electricity pylons. (IWM MH24430)

selection was shifted toward vulnerable parts of the German war economy like ball bearing production, then against German transport and communication links prior to and during the Allied invasion of Europe. SOE also played an important role in hindering Germany's attempt to build an atomic bomb by sabotaging the production of heavy water in Norway. On the night of 27/28 February 1944, a team of ten SOE-trained Norwegian commandos broke into the Vemork plant at Rjukan. They temporarily disrupted production and later sank the ferry on Lake Tinnsjo carrying the remaining stocks of heavy water as it was transferred to Germany.

Above all, SOE is perhaps most famous for organizing attacks on the European railway system. We have already described the basics of sabotage, the use of PE and fog signals to blow up trains. This was just the tip of the iceberg. Although blowing up locomotives and bridges was spectacular and good for the morale of local resisters, the Nazi rail system through Europe was extremely robust. It was far better for agents to target the cranes used for clearing derailed trains, or the turntables at depots, or even the hearts of rail points. These were the real weak spots of the transport network and became harder and harder to replace.

Ingenious methods were found to introduce explosives to the target. In one case explosives were camouflaged as lumps of coal. When a stoker scooped up the charge it would explode in the furnace with devastating effect. The use of such devices also had an important psychological effect, making stokers literally too scared to work. On similar lines, another scheme saw SOE fill the carcasses of dead rats with PE and a fuse. A consignment of the rats was sent to Europe, but the aircraft carrying them came down over Belgium. The Germans grew suspicious about the rats and discovered the ploy. An alert was put out to be on the guard for rats in coal bunkers. The mission was not a total failure, however, as Gestapo HQs were inundated with thousands of dead rats that people believed might contain explosives.

Other than the use of explosive charges, a different method of sabotaging trains was to flatten the lubricating pipes with a hammer blow, or to stuff rags into pipes and cause a blockage. Another method was to apply an abrasive like

 OPERATION *GUNNERSIDE*

One of the most famous operations of the war was the attack on the Norsk-Hydro heavy water plant at Vemork on the night of 27/28 February 1943. Heavy water was needed for the production of plutonium and so the loss of the plant held up the German nuclear bomb project indefinitely. After a long ski journey, the party of ten saboteurs approached the plant by climbing down a ravine the Germans had considered impassable. After cutting the padlock to a gate, the saboteurs rushed into the plant and began setting explosive charges on the cylinders containing the heavy water. A Norwegian night watchman was found and held at gunpoint. Just as the team were about to set 30-second fuses, the night watchman asked them to wait while he went and collected his spectacles. With war shortages he said he would be unlikely to find new ones. The saboteurs agreed to wait. Once the charges were set, the team left a Thompson submachine gun behind to show that this had been the work of regular commandos, not an act of resistance by the local population that might result in hostage-taking or reprisal killings.

Emery powder into lubricating oil used on wheel axles. As the axles began to turn they would begin to heat and expand, locking-up miles from where the sabotage took place. The most famous use of this technique came in June 1944, when SOE used abrasive grease on the rolling stock earmarked for taking 2nd SS Panzer Division 'Das Reich' to Normandy. While the wagons were in sidings, members of the resistance applied the oil: after 50–100km (31–62 miles) the trains began to pack up and were abandoned by the SS, who took to the roads. Such untraceable acts drove the Germans mad with rage and, when there was no culprit to blame, they lashed out at random against the civilian population. Sadly, many innocent civilians were murdered or were incarcerated as hostages; but for every martyr, resentment against the Nazis grew.

Other than railways, a key sabotage target was the German U-boat fleet. With the submarine bases heavily defended, SOE developed platinum pills that could attack the batteries used to allow submarines to operate submerged. These pills could be added locally, or at the factories in which the batteries were constructed. There were also indirect methods to attack the U-boats, and depress the morale of the already beleaguered crews even further. The pods of the Mucuna plant are covered in coarse hairs that cause itchiness and blisters when they come into contact with the skin. Disguising the powder as talc, SOE provided it to a resistance group in Troyes that managed to infiltrate a laundry and have the powder sprinkled on the freshly laundered shirts of U-boat crews. It is commonly believed at least one U-boat crew was forced to return to port thinking they were suffering from acute dermatitis. In Norway, the resistance went a step further when supplied with the powder. They put it into condoms which they then repackaged and sold at good profit to brothels catering for German servicemen in Trondheim.

SOE also targeted the food stocks of the U-boat fleet. German submariners often supplemented their tinned rations with luxury foodstuffs bought on the black market. These unofficial victuals could be doctored by resistance agents before being sold. It was found, for example, that a few drops of kerosene added into olive oil would give off an almighty stink when opened and ways were worked out to contaminate the Germans' beer. Methyl telluride was added to rice, making it smell of garlic; cheese was infected with mould and vermin infestations encouraged. As if this was not bad enough, SOE experimented with a form of 'stink bomb' to embarrass and upset in equal measure. This was a chemical that was sprayed onto servicemen in public places. In a similar vein, away from U-boats, powerful laxatives were administered to a party of Italian senior officers by doctoring their wine. Although such measures might appear small and insignificant, they made life frustrating and uncomfortable for enemy troops.

Training for industrial sabotage missions was extensive and wide ranging. Agents had to be comfortable with the machines and installations they might face and be able to feel their way around them in the dark. Knowledge of the workings would reveal their weakest points. Often it was not necessary to blow up an entire plant or engine, only to knock out one vital, hard-to-replace component. Students were therefore taken to inspect similar machinery in British factories or, if this was not possible, wooden or metal replicas were constructed.

Detailed plans of the target factories were provided, along with intelligence on the guard routines. Dummy runs were set up, with trainers enacting the role of guards. Breaking into factories was as much an art as the sabotage itself. SOE agents learned how to scale fences and walls, negotiate barbed wire and circumvent, or eliminate, sentries. At the end of their training students were sent off with false British ID cards and papers allowing them to get work in a munitions works. They would have to bring back secret plans or plant dummy charges on a piece of plant to prove they had got past the guards. Half an hour after this exercise began the local police force would be contacted and told a parachutist had landed and was believed to be a German agent. Such exercises gave some indication of the realities of life in the field as a saboteur.

Wireless Operators

The first SOE radio operator to transmit from occupied Europe was Odd Starheim. Operating under the codename 'Cheese', Starheim landed in Norway in January 1941. He even managed to radio out information about the first sighting of the *Bismarck* as it went on its maiden voyage. More famous is the first radio operator in France, Georges Bégué, who landed near Châteauroux on the night of 5 May 1941.

SOE officer operating a B2 portable radio set in Macedonia, August 1944. One of the key functions of SOE was to put local resistance groups in touch with Allied High Command. (IWM HU67333)

It is often said that all subsequent radio operators were named George and given a numerical suffix (George II, George III etc.) honouring this Gallic pioneer. There are others who believe this numbering system originated at Pratt's gentlemen's club in London, where the waiters were all known as George on account of the doddery patrons being unable to remember the staff's names.

Wireless operators were the linchpin of their networks. Typically of the internal politics SOE faced, when it was created SOE was not permitted to manage its own signals traffic, codes or operating schedules. These remained the prerogative of MI6's Section VIII. This arrangement remained until 1 June 1942 when the head of MI6, Sir Stuart Menzies, unexpectedly allowed SOE to assume responsibility for its own affairs. The first step in creating a wireless service was to set up a chain of Home Stations across the globe. By the end of the war there were three in Britain (around Grendon and

Close-up of the B2 transmitter developed by SOE technicians for uniformed 'Jedburgh' parties, which were parachuted to assist resistance groups after D-Day. The Morse key can be seen on the bottom right. (IWM HU56738)

Poundon in Buckinghamshire); four in the Mediterranean (Algeria, Cairo, Gibraltar and Malta); three in Africa (Freetown, Lagos and Durban) and three in the Far East (India, Ceylon and Australia). Each of these stations was like a giant switchboard exchange, plugged into an armada of wireless masts pointing deep into enemy territory.

The Home Stations were staffed by hundreds of girls not old enough for industrial conscription (below 20 years old) who had been recruited by Ministry of Labour or the First Aid Nursing Yeomanry (FANY) organization. The girls were trained as radio operators and coders by SOE at STS54(a) (Fawley Court, Henley) in batches of up to 150 at a time. Very security-conscious and hardworking, these young women held the fate of many agents in their hands and felt a definite bond between them.

Each radio operator in the field had a strict operating schedule to prevent the Home Stations from being swamped with traffic. The scheduling was very tight and the Home Station would only listen in for five minutes before closing down. At the allotted time, a Home Station operator would put on headphones and sit by the set with pen and notepaper ready to transcribe the encoded message. At the beginning of every signal, the operator would switch on a recording device. The main purpose of this device was to keep a record of the original signal, should the message somehow turn out to be garbled. Perhaps more importantly, if there was any suspicion that the Germans had taken over the set, the recording could be scientifically compared to ones made during the agent's training to see if it matched. Every radio operator had a different style of tapping out Morse code. Some elongated certain dots or dashes in certain letters and no two 'hands' were the same. This signature was very hard to mimic.

Young FANYs trained by SOE as wireless operators maintaining contact with agents throughout Europe.
As a general rule, agents transmitted through the day, while replies were sent out between 2100hrs and midnight. It was impressed upon the girls that the agents in the field were working under intense pressure and might make errors in their transmissions. The sign on the wall gave ample reminder to get the message right first time and not to keep the agent on the air any more than necessary. (IWM HU32841)

The radio operator would be trained to send a message of up to 600 letters (120 groups of five letters) in five minutes. If the operator needed to send a longer message, he or she would often cycle through an agreed change of frequencies midway through the transmission. It was important that the Home Station operator kept up with all this and took the messages down correctly. The girls were told that the agent might be under enormous stress when sending these messages and the worst thing they could do was ask the radio operator to resend the whole message because they had made a mistake.

Another set of FANYs in what appears to be a typing pool at one of SOE's Home Stations. (IWM HU47913)

Once the message was received, it was sent to a coder. The messages would be deciphered and sent off to the respective country sections for action. Frustratingly they were often indecipherable, either through atmospheric interference, or by the agent making a mistake enciphering the message in the first place. As a result thousands of man-hours were spent trying to work out the meaning of messages from the field.

To reduce the risks as much as possible, radio operators in the field had to undergo extensive training at STS 52 (Thame Park). The six-week course was extremely laborious and included a visit to an outstation (STS 52b at Dunbar), where long-distance signalling was practised in realistic conditions. There was also a 14-day security briefing at Beaulieu before the course culminated in the radio operators being sent on a dummy run into a British city. Armed with a radio set, they were told to find lodgings, set up the transmitter and begin sending signals without being caught by the security services.

Before embarking on a mission, each clandestine radio operator would normally be assigned to a leader or group. In terms of arriving behind enemy lines, their instructions and training were no different from other SOE agents. Once they arrived in the occupied territories, however, they had to isolate themselves quickly from the rest of the group for their mutual protection. Communication between the chief and his radio operator was to be through cut-outs only. Because the threat of capture was so real, the leader of the group would have to keep all membership, plans and hiding places secret from the operator. On the flip side, the radio operator would locate his own safe houses and recruit his own look-outs without their being known by the chief.

Ideally, the radio operator would have several sets concealed in a variety of safe houses away from where he resided. The chosen transmission sites had to have a clear signal to the Home Station, which made urban centres difficult places from which to operate. Another hazard of urban centres was the presence of structural steel girders in the building. It was found that the metal frame of the building would amplify the key click on the Morse code transmitter and would be heard in neighbouring rooms. It must be remembered that only a minority of people were involved in resistance activity and therefore suspicious behaviour or noises might result in a police investigation.

Once a good site was located, the operator would find a hiding place for the set. Most sets were disguised as suitcases, but some were hidden in gramophone players, which made them easier to conceal. When leaving the hiding place after transmission, the operator was instructed to leave no trace of clandestine activity and to destroy any coded messages. He was also to set little traps to see if the set was disturbed in his absence – for example, placing a leaf in the keyhole, or a hair across a door.

The operator was given set times during the day when the Home Station would be listening out for him. This schedule meant he had to have an alibi for going to the hiding place in case stopped en route, or if the building was searched. The operator was told never to carry a gun in public, or to engage in any other clandestine activities. He was to recruit his own watchmen and always place lookouts while operating. Above all, he was to have a secondary escape route if disturbed.

The first SOE radio operators were encumbered by the Mark XV transceiver, which had been designed for MI6 use in 1936. The set came with a separate transmitter and receiver, each packed into a heavy wooden case. Weighing 44lb (20kg) it was not exactly ideal for the purposes SOE had in mind. SOE therefore developed its own sets at a series of radio workshops (STN VII) located variously at Wembley, Watford and Birmingham. The design brief was to reduce the size and weight of the Mark XV set without losing anything in terms of power or signal strength. Recognizing the need for the set to be easily concealed, there was a further stipulation that the new set had to fit inside an ordinary continental suitcase.

The first solution was the Mark II Suitcase Transceiver, which comprised three separate units each 11in × 4in × 3in (28cm × 10cm × 7.6cm) in size, containing the transmitter, a receiver and a battery pack. All three units were packed into a suitably weathered suitcase as required and at 20lb (9kg) weighed less than half the SIS set. Further improvements led to the introduction of the 3 Mark II, or B2 set, which was one of the most popular sets used by agents in the field. The key advantage of the B2 set was an in-built 6-volt battery that allowed the operator to quickly switch from mains to battery power if necessary. This ability was an important feature in thwarting the German detection procedures. The Germans had powerful direction finding (DF) antennae that could be used to triangulate the source of the radio signal to within a few miles. If this happened to be in a town, the Germans could narrow the source down by pulling the mains power from a particular quarter. If the clandestine transmission stopped suddenly, the Germans would know the agent was operating in the area of the power cut and house-to-house searches would commence. The ability of the B2 set, in allowing the radio operator to quickly switch to battery power, negated this German tactic.

Even then the Germans had a number of techniques for locating 'pianists', as clandestine radio operators were often known. The first measure was a ban on all private transmitters. By making any form of radio ham activity illegal, the airwaves were left relatively uncluttered except for military traffic. Snap controls at railway stations and busy street intersections were set up in the hunt for sets being transported between hiding places. Meanwhile, mobile DF stations were hidden in delivery vans and ambulances, and hand-held devices and even aircraft hovering overhead could

Interior of the Radio Communications Division factory, STN VIIa, near Wembley. Production of radios began here in June 1942 and continued until the German V1 flying bomb offensive forced production to move to Birmingham in 1944. The sets produced by SOE were far lighter than those initially provided by MI6. (IWM HU56752)

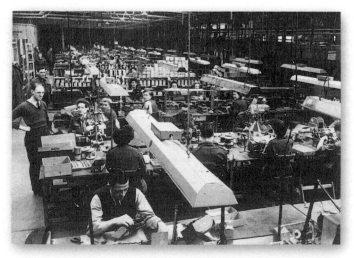

Partisans charging a radio battery with a hand-operated dynamo, Macedonia, July 1944. (IWM HU67330)

all help pinpoint the exact source to a street or house. If the Germans got lucky, they could quickly erect barricades and then close in.

The best way of avoiding German DF was for the operator to stay on air as little as possible. Unfortunately, there were so few radio operators available in the field they were often overloaded with work, forced to stay on the air too long and therefore became more susceptible to discovery. They were also handicapped by the rigid system of fixed call times. If the Germans heard a radio at 1505hrs on Monday, they knew there was a good chance it would come back on the air the same time the following day and they would already be listening in. If the radio operator kept broadcasting from the same location, day after day, it was only a matter of time before the front door opened and a squad of Nazis swooped in. To alleviate this problem, SOE began introducing a more flexible system in which the radio operator would not repeat their call time for four months.

Each operator also had an emergency frequency that was monitored constantly. The operator would tap out his call sign and establish contact. In return the Home Station would acknowledge and stand by for the message to be transmitted. The message was then turned into plain text by the cipher clerk and then forwarded to SOE HQ at Baker Street, where it would be considered. A reply was sent back to the Home Station, where it would be encoded, broken into groups of five letters and transmitted back to the agent. This whole process could easily take more than an hour, so if the agent remained on the air waiting for the response, they were very prone to detection.

A bicycle has been fitted with a pedal generator to charge the batteries of a wireless set. (IWM HU56739)

If taken alive, the radio operator could attempt to bargain his life by agreeing to work under German control. To warn SOE that this had occurred, agents had special security checks they inserted into the text.

Jacqueline Nearne demonstrating a typical Morse training session. The signals sergeant listens to the signal attentively though headphones while the student transmits a message from a written sheet. Even at its peak, SOE was turning out fewer than 16–18 radio operators a month. In the field they were worth their weight in gold, but they were extremely vulnerable to capture. In fact, the average radio operator had a life expectancy of six weeks to three months. (IWM MH24440)

Each agent had two checks: the first was a 'bluff' they could tell the Germans, the second was something known only to them and their controllers in London. For instance, they might incorrectly spell the third word of each message, or insert a random letter. If the security check was omitted, in theory SOE ought to realize and, in an attempt to prolong the agent's life, they could play along with the charade, passing the Germans just enough information to keep them interested in keeping the agent alive.

Of course, humans being humans, the security check system did not always go to plan. Agents frequently forgot to use the checks, and the Home Stations grew equally lax in insisting upon them. Although a set was played back in France, the biggest catastrophe of SOE's existence occurred in Holland. A W/T operator was captured and so omitted his security code. The Dutch Section should have been alarmed that the security checks were missing, but they carried on as normal and 43 agents were captured. It was only when two Dutch agents escaped and came back to England that they confirmed the Germans were operating the radio set and all the agents sent since then had been arrested on landing. The episode was so controversial the Dutch wondered if it was a conspiracy of some kind on SOE's behalf.

THE MISSION

SOE agents were often recruited with a specific mission in mind. With their training complete, this mission was at last revealed. Mission types generally broke down into two types: an in-and-out objective, where the agent would be called upon to perform a single specific attack or task; and longer term objectives, where the agent would be required to live behind enemy lines for an indefinite period.

In all cases, the first stage of the mission was to select a team capable of performing the task. The leader would preferably be someone with experience in previous missions. Around him would be added the radio operator, couriers and weapons trainers – whatever was felt necessary. The leader was consulted about the other team members, as it was vital the team had a good chemistry and were comfortable with trusting their lives in each other's hands. Once the team was selected, all of them were briefed in every facet of the mission in case there were casualties.

SOE's principal aim was to foster resistance in the occupied territories. In order not to provoke savage retaliation against the civilian population, SOE spent much of its energy creating a so-called Secret Army. This was a body of resistance fighters who would remain passive until the Allied invasion called upon them to act. Conserving their strength until the vital moment, the Secret Army would tie up German reinforcements at the time the Allies needed the most help. These armies had to be recruited, equipped, trained, supplied and led – all under the noses of German garrisons. In order to preserve the strength of the group, many agents spent much of their time trying to prevent resisters from striking out too early.

There were, of course, numerous sabotage missions, some of which have already been discussed. At this point the complicated relationship between SOE and the RAF should be mentioned. Aerial bombardment in the 1940s was not a precision instrument. It was often the case that bombs fell off-target and killed civilians in the occupied countries. Such attacks alienated SOE agents from the very people they needed to provide them with shelter and sustenance. SOE argued that an agent armed with a backpack filled with PE might obtain a level of precision which the RAF could only dream of. Naturally the RAF was not convinced by this argument.

A solution to the problem came after a successful sabotage attack on the Peugeot factory on 5 November 1943. Following a messy RAF attack,

Display of parachute containers from the General Equipment Department at STN XVb's demonstration room in the Natural History Museum. On the podium are three Type C containers and one Type H container (right) showing the different types of seasonal camouflage employed. (IWM HU61138)

SOE agent Henri Rée contacted Rudolphe Peugeot and promised to keep Bomber Command away if he agreed to sabotage his own factory. Peugeot agreed and there were no further air attacks. Using this as a model, on 20 December the RAF agreed to allow SOE a fixed time period on certain targets to 'do a blackmail job' before they sent the bombers in.

To provide proof that the targets had been successfully attacked, an SOE operative would visit the plant the morning after posing as an insurance assessor. In this guise he would diligently take photographs of the damaged machines, bid good day and leave. The films were then smuggled out to Switzerland and from there to London for analysis. If the SOE team failed, then the bombers would be sent in. In other cases, if the security was tight, SOE might call up an air raid to create confusion, during which they could infiltrate a plant, set their explosives and leave. If the SOE operatives were lucky, the Germans would think the damage had been caused by the air raid and thus reprisals against the local population were less likely.

Heydrich assassins Josef Gabcik (left) and Jan Kubis (right). After extensive paramilitary training at the hands of SOE instructors, Gabcik and Kubis were hand-picked for the task. Trained by SOE, these two agents were part of a larger team sent to kill Heydrich. They were parachuted into Czechoslovakia armed with submachine guns, grenades, a range of explosives, a mortar and a lethal hypodermic needle. Both were unmarried orphans and both volunteered knowing there was little chance of survival. After completing their mission, they were cornered by the SS in a Prague church. They chose suicide rather than surrender. (IWM HU47370/ HU47372)

Less well-known than its sabotage operations, SOE carried out or planned a number of assassination missions against high-profile figures. As early as March 1941, SOE planned to assassinate SS chief Heinrich Himmler on a visit to Oslo. The plan failed due to a programme change, but the following year SOE scored a success with Operation *Anthropoid* when it trained a group of Czechoslovakian agents to assassinate Himmler's deputy, Reinhart Heydrich, in Prague. It is widely believed that SOE was also involved in the assassination of the Vichy French admiral François Darlan in 1942. The French assassin worked for SOE and used an SOE-issued pistol, but his act was not officially sanctioned.

With the organization suffering at the hands of German counter-espionage agencies, several attempts were made to go on the offensive and attack known Gestapo officials and collaborators. The first plan was known as 'Execution Month', which was scheduled for October 1943. The idea was to target German officials and send them death warrants at the end of the summer.

Reinhard Heydrich's Mercedes Type 320 after the assassination attempt. The damage to the door from the Gammon grenade thrown by Gabcik can be seen clearly. (IWM HU47379)

Then, as the winter closed in, SOE agents would begin a killing spree. A thousand Welrod silent pistols were ordered to be ready by the end of August with 100 every month after. At the last minute, however, SOE cancelled this mission because of the fear of reprisals against civilians. Yet with the invasion of Europe drawing nearer, at the end of February 1944 Operation *Ratweek* took place. Details are sketchy, but it is known that attacks were made in France, Belgium, Holland, Denmark and Norway. In France, a driver working for SOE's ARMADA circuit accounted for 11 Gestapo officers in Lyon alone.

Most intriguing of all was a 1944 plan to assassinate Hitler codenamed Operation *Foxley*. After D-Day some Allied commanders were concerned that the Germans were fighting on solely because of Hitler: remove Hitler, they said, and the war would end. Numerous ways of killing Hitler were discussed, including blowing up his train, or poisoning his water supply. These were overlooked in favour of a sniper shooting him at his Bavarian retreat, in Berchtesgaden. While some believed Hitler's death would end the war, others believed he was such an incompetent strategist he was an indirect asset to the Allies. With hindsight, although the chance of success was extremely slim, if the mission had gone ahead and the opportunity had been taken, there might not have been a German Ardennes offensive in December 1944; the war might therefore have finished sooner, and countless persons might have been spared in the Nazi death camps.

SOE was also known to resort to kidnapping as a means of eliminating certain enemy targets. On 26 April 1944, the German commander of the 22nd Infantry Division in Crete, Generalmajor Kreipe was abducted by an SOE team while being driven to his villa. After a detailed stakeout, Major 'Paddy' Leigh-Fermor and Captain 'Billy' Moss dressed as German MPs and flagged down Kreipe's car on a hairpin turn. After hitting the driver over the head with a cosh, they pulled guns on the general and pushed him into the back of the car. With Paddy wearing the general's hat, the car passed through a succession of German roadblocks, with accompanying salutes. The general's car was ditched by the coast in an attempt to make the Germans think the party had escaped by submarine. In fact, the

A selection of 9mm Welrod pistols – a silent killing weapon developed by SOE at STN IX (Welwyn). The magazine-stock could be removed, making the weapon very easy to conceal. Hundreds were ordered in advance of 'Execution Month' in June 1943 to assassinate German officials. (IWM HU56779)

The Welwand 'sleeve gun' was just 12in (30.5cm) long and fired a single .22-cal bullet with an effective range of 10ft (3m). A lanyard was attached to the rear of the gun and through the sleeve to the agent's belt. The agent would approach close to the target, lower the lanyard, put the barrel against the target's back and fire by pushing a switch on top of the barrel. (IWM HU56777)

local garrison did not take the bait and a manhunt ensued. Aided by Cretan partisans, the SOE team evaded capture for 20 days. On 16 May, after a gruelling trek, the SOE team were met by a British motor-launch on a deserted beach to the south of the island. Kreipe was taken to Cairo and spent the rest of the war in embarrassed captivity. Moss and Leigh-Fermor were awarded the Distinguished Service Order (DSO).

The Briefing

The mission briefing was the last chance to acquaint the agent properly with all the information available and to pre-empt, as much as possible, every eventuality that might arise in the coming mission. This meant that the country sections had to trawl for clues on how German occupation had changed the countries they were operating in. In an area subject to rationing and tight police controls, the number of passes and coupons required to exist were astounding. The country section pieced this information together from snippets out of foreign newspapers and radio programmes, from interviews with refugees and from returning agents. Each new piece of information had to be passed on to the next batch of agents lest they were caught out by a change in procedure.

For the agents, the first stage of the briefing process was to fix their cover stories. The agent had to learn and believe this cover story implicitly, training himself always to react 'in character'. The agents were even taught not to think in English lest they slipped up. To make the fateful mistake of accidentally replying in English could spell doom. Sometimes, of course, despite every attempt to hide their true identity, a local would guess who they were. In 1942 SOE officer 'Monty' Woodhouse was part of the 'Harling' mission sent to blow up the Gorgopotamos railway viaduct in Greece. Having spent a number of weeks perfecting his Greek accent and living in the hills as a shepherd, he went into a local town. When he arrived the bus driver tapped him on the shoulder and said to him: 'Eh, British, if you haven't got anywhere to stay, I've got a spare room!'

To try to avoid such situations, meticulous attention to detail went into preparing the best possible cover. Using as much truth and personal knowledge

HEYDRICH'S ASSASSINATION

On 27 May 1942, Reinhart Heydrich was being driven from his home to Prague Castle in a Mercedes-Benz. Travelling without his usual police escort, his driver was forced to slow down on a hairpin bend. Waiting for him were two SOE-trained assassins and a third who acted as a lookout. As the car slowed, Josef Gabcik walked out in front of the car with a Sten gun hidden beneath his overcoat: the gun jammed when he tried to open fire. Instead of speeding off, Heydrich ordered his driver to stop. As he drew his pistol to shoot Gabcik the second assassin, Jan Kubis, threw a Gammon grenade at the car. It fell short of the open-top car and exploded in the gutter by the rear passenger door. Standing up in his seat, Heydrich was wounded by fragments from the explosion. As the assassins ran away, Heydrich tried to give chase. He went to hospital, where the wound became infected and he died on 4 June. A potential successor to Hitler, Heydrich was head of the SS secret service, the *Reichssicherheitshauptamt* (Reich Security Head Office; RHSA), and was one of the principle architects of the Holocaust. Edvard Benes, leader of the Czechoslovakian government-in-exile, had ordered the assassination because the ruthless Heydrich was successfully exploiting the country's industrial potential for the benefit of the Nazi war machine. He also wanted the world to see that free Czechoslovakians were contributing to the Allied cause. This stance came at a terrible price. When Heydrich died of his wounds, retribution was swift and brutal, culminating in the obliteration of the town of Lidice where all the men over 16 were shot, the women sent to Ravensbrück concentration camp, and the children given up for adoption.

A typical mission briefing. Scale models have been created to show agents the area in which they will be operating and how to best approach the intended target. Although SOE was not an intelligence-gathering agency, considerable effort went into researching and planning missions to give the agents the best possible chance of success and survival. (IWM MH24448)

as possible, each agent would be given a new identity, with a past stretching back to imaginary grandparents, aunts, uncles, cousins and so on. To thwart the research of enemy authorities, the agents were assigned birthplaces in remote villages or on overseas colonial possessions, or in towns whose town halls had been bombed and where the records had been destroyed,. Male agents in particular also had to have plausible immunity from military or labour service. In many cases this meant finding them jobs among sympathetic bosses, which in turn meant giving agents work experience in British firms in order to familiarize them with their cover profession.

Many agents were required to work undercover, but a large number wore their uniforms and made no attempt to blend in. This was particularly true in parts of Greece, Albania and Yugoslavia. Yet where agents had to operate in areas tightly controlled by the Germans – and this applied to about half of the agents sent abroad – the next step was to ensure they were dressed authentically. A panel of experts examined the agent. Physical traits like English hairstyles were changed and excessive hair lacquer removed. British and European dentistry techniques were also different: if the agent had a filling, this would be removed and replaced with a gold plug after the continental fashion.

The agents received a wardrobe of clothes authentic to the area they were sent to operate in. As a general rule, clothes could not appear British in design. British laundry marks had to be removed, labels changed and so on. Refugees arriving in Britain had their clothing taken away. Specialist tailors would then unpick the clothes and make patterns so they might be copied. European tailors and seamstresses were recruited from among the refugees and set to work on manufacturing the clothes. Thousands of articles were produced and were available off-the-peg to men going on missions. Because local fashions for women were so changeable, female agents received a bespoke service.

For agents returning on a second mission there was always the problem that they might be recognized and so had to disguise their physical characteristics completely. By changing hairstyles, clothes, wearing spectacles, shaving off or growing a beard or a moustache, or by adopting a different posture, the agent could hope to foil investigators. In more extreme cases, if an agent had become known to the Gestapo, SOE could arrange for a plastic surgeon.

Agents would receive a set of false identity papers created by expert criminal forgers recommended to SOE by Scotland Yard. Each agent had to check his new identity papers and ensure the names and dates were correct, and familiarize himself with the different documents, along with the local currency. He was then told to break his clothes and shoes in before going on a mission. More than a few neglected to do this and bitterly regretted it when they arrived in the field wearing shiny new, uncreased clothes.

Agents then had to consider what equipment to take with them and what they would discard after landing. As basic kit, an agent might need a map, torch, compass, first aid kit, knife and flask. He would certainly need a shovel to bury his parachute and overalls. He might also need a pistol in case the landing was opposed. Beyond that, however, a pistol might become an embarrassment for an agent who had to pass through tight controls.

Members of the British SOE liaison mission to the Cetnik partisans, Yugoslavia, during the winter of 1942–43. (IWM HU56053)

Agents also had access to a number of drugs that would help them on their mission. These included 'A' tablets for airsickness; 'B' pills containing Benzedrine for use as a stimulant (the amphetamine Mecrodrin was also issued); the 'E' pill: a quick-working anaesthetic that would knock a person out for 30 seconds; 'K' pills for inducing sleep; and the 'L' (lethal) pill, a lethal dose of cyanide. The suicide pills worked quickest when sucked and dissolved in the mouth. Death, the scientists assured, would be painless and come within 30 seconds. If the tablet was swallowed and ingested in the stomach, death might take up to five minutes. The actual pill was quite small and could be concealed in a ring, hidden in a wine cork or, for female agents, in a lipstick. Others were given an insoluble coating and could be carried safely

Partisan hideout. Here uniformed SOE officers sort out parachutes after a container drop. In theory parachutes were meant to be destroyed, but in practice their material was highly valued and put to numerous uses, including bedding. (IWM HU67322)

in the mouth: when required the agent would have to bite through the coating to release the active chemical inside.

The final part of the briefing was to hand the agent his Operation Instructions. These would set out the exact goals of the mission, providing the agent with his codename, the details of other team members and any local passwords necessary for making contact with the reception committee. The instructions would also contain details of coded messages he might expect to hear broadcast on the BBC, and they provided cover addresses if anything went wrong. The agent also received a certain amount of cash to fund resistance activities. In total F Section sent 316,947,000 Francs with agents on air operations alone. Working on an unofficial exchange rate of 200 Francs to the pound, this amounts to more than £1.5 million given to agents. Theoretically the agents could dip into this pot of money, but, as many German agents found to their cost, an extravagant agent courting the finer things in life would soon suffer the consequences.

All that remained was for the agent to make the necessary arrangements: a will and letters to loved ones. Unlike regular army soldiers who could send and receive mail from relatives and loved ones, SOE agents had to remain completely incommunicado. In the worst case, if an agent's death was confirmed it was doubly hard to inform the parents. Although as much was done as possible to explain the circumstances of their passing, operational security meant details were rarely given away. In the regular army, relatives could expect a message of consolation from the commanding officer or a comrade, in which the value of their son's or daughter's sacrifice could be made clear. In SOE the most any next of kin could reasonably expect was a letter asking them to come and collect the deceased's belongings. To alleviate the natural anxieties of losing touch, SOE sections would make arrangements for keeping the agents' next of kin informed they were safe. In F Section, steps were taken so that birthday and Christmas presents were bought and delivered on the agent's behalf. In one extreme example, the section proposed to a girl on behalf of one agent who had been sent abroad without having had the chance to pop the question himself. Her acceptance was signalled back to the agent, along with the demand for a suitable engagement ring.

Departure

After listlessly waiting for the right phase of the moon and for clear weather over the drop zone, the nod to go ahead must have come as a relief and a

THE PARACHUTE DROP

Although some agents were secreted into Europe by submarine, boat, or even flown in by Lysander or Hudson, the parachute drop was the most common means of entry behind enemy lines. Jumps were often made from as low as 500–650ft (150–200m), so the agents had their ankles bandaged and rubber pads inserted into a set of specially designed overalls nicknamed 'striptease suits'. Once in the aircraft, the agents were given the opportunity to snatch a few hours rest before the drop-zone was reached, and sleeping bags were provided by the crew. As the drop-zone approached, the crew would stir the agents and offer them coffee and sandwiches. The dispatcher would attach the static lines to their parachutes. Most parachute jumps were made from specially converted Halifax bombers. To facilitate jumping, the underside gun turret was removed forming a hatch about 1m (3ft 3in) in diameter. The agents would sit around the open hatch waiting for the 'green light'. The dispatcher lowered his right arm as a signal to jump and yelled at the top of his voice 'GO!' As the agents jumped, their equipment would be pushed out in panniers or cylindrical containers. Only a few seconds later, the agents were on the ground, gathering their parachutes and hoping their arrival had been unseen.

SOE operative William Pickering in a 'striptease' parachute suit and harness. These zip-up overalls protected the agent's civilian clothes in rough landings. The agent was also further protected by ankle bindings, knee pads and a rubber spine pad. (IWM HU48173)

cause for anxiety. Outwardly at least, the news appears to have been a cause for celebration with most agents. They would be treated to a slap-up meal with their comrades before an RAF station wagon arrived, which the agents called 'the hearse'. On the doorstep of the country section's holding apartment, there would be handshakes and the customary good luck messages – F Section always using a certain Gallic expletive in a gesture of good-humoured defiance.

Once in the hands of the RAF, the agents (or 'bods' as the airmen called their passengers) were taken to the aerodrome. The RAF had two principal 'special duties' squadrons – 138 and 161 based in Bedfordshire. There was another based at Tangmere in Sussex, which 161 Squadron used for pick-up missions by Lysander and Hudson aircraft. As the agents were driven to the airfield it must have been a slightly unreal sensation that in three or four hours they would be in Nazi-held territory. It was a quiet time for the agent interspersed with a chain of cigarettes.

Taken to a quiet part of the base away from prying eyes, the agents were searched for anything that might blow their cover. After looking for stray coins and bus tickets, the agent's pockets would be brushed out. There would be one last briefing, as quite often part of the mission plan would be changed at the very last minute. The section head would go through the mission details one final time and wish the agent good luck. The head of F Section then gave his agents a parting gift, normally a pair of gold cufflinks, or a gold powder compact for female agents. The gift was a reminder of their comrades back in England and, more practically, their commercial value meant they could be pawned if the agent became hard-up for cash. They would share a final toast before being helped

A rare photograph from April 1943 of an SOE team about to board a Halifax bomber bound for a mission in Albania. The photograph was taken at Derna airfield, Tripolitania, in North Africa. (IWM HU64928)

into their parachute overalls and harnesses. After a brief introduction to the captain and crew, the agents were taken out to the waiting aircraft. Often there would be a farewell party of Wrens who would ask the agents for their autographs before they were shoved up into the belly of a Halifax bomber with their equipment. With the deafening roar of the engines, they would feel the aircraft accelerate down the runway. Then it was off into darkening skies and the unknown.

APPENDICES

SOE F SECTION CIRCUITS IN FRANCE 1941–44

AUTOGIRO*	Mar 41 – Aug 42	BRICKLAYER*	Nov 42 – Feb 44	WIZARD ᵛ	Mar 44 – Jul 44
VENTRILOQUIST * ᵛ	May 41 – Nov 42	MUSICIAN*	Nov 42 – Aug 44	LIONTAMER*	Mar 44
FACADE/ TILLEUL* ᵛ	Aug 41 – Jul 42	FARMER* ᵛ	Nov 42 – Aug 44	BARGEE*	Mar 44
HECKLER/ SAINT ᵛ	Aug 41 – Jul 42	BOOKMAKER	Dec 42 – Mar 43	MINISTER* ᵛ	Mar 44 – Sep 44
TINKER ᵛ	Aug 41 – Nov 42	FARRIER	Jan 43 – Apr 44	MASON ᵛ	Mar 44 – Aug 44
URCHIN*	Sep 41 – Nov 43	CINEMA-PHONO*	Jan 43 – Jul 44	TUTOR	Mar 44
SPRUCE/ GARDENER ᵛ	Sep 41 – Aug 44	STATIONER*	Jan 43 – Apr 44	FIREMAN ᵛ	Mar 44 – Sep 44
CARTE	Sep 41 – Mar 43	JOCKEY* ᵛ	Mar 43 – Aug 44	ROVER*	Mar 44 – May 44
CORSICAN*	Sep 41 – Mar 43	PUBLICAN*	Feb 43 – Sep 43	SCHOLAR*	Mar 44 – Jun 44
SPINDLE*	Oct 41 – Sep 42	SALESMAN ᵛ	Apr 43 – Aug 44	HISTORIAN* ᵛ	Apr 44 – Aug 44
PROFESSOR-PEDLAR ᵛ	Jan 42 – June 43	STOCKBROKER ᵛ	Apr 44 – Sep 44	BEGGAR ᵛ	Apr 44 – Aug 44
PRUNUS*	Feb 42 – Aug 43	SCULLION	Apr 43 – Aug 43	TREASURER ᵛ	Apr 44 – Sep 44
PLANE	Apr 42 – Apr 43	PARSON*	Jun 43 – Feb 44	CARVER ᵛ	Apr 44 – Sep 44
CHESTNUT*	Apr 42 – Aug 43	SACRISTAN ᵛ	Jun 43 – Sep 44	LABOURER*	Apr 44 – Jun 44
SATIRIST	Jun 42 – Aug 43	MONK*	Jun 43 – Mar 43	RACKETEER ᵛ	Apr 44 – Aug 44
DETECTIVE* ᵛ	Jun 42 – Aug 44	ARCHDEACON*	Jun 43	FREELANCE ᵛ	Apr 44 – Sep 44
PRIVET*	Jul 42 – Jun 43	ACOLYTE ᵛ	Jun 43 – Sep 44	SHIPWRIGHT ᵛ	May 44 – Sep 44
MARKSMAN* ᵛ	Jul 42 – Aug 44	DRESSMAKER	Aug 43 – Sep 43	WRESTLER ᵛ	May 44 – Sep 44
DONKEYMAN* ᵛ	Jun 42 – Aug 44	AUTHOR/ DIGGER* ᵛ	Sep 43 – Aug 44	DIETICIAN ᵛ	May 44 – Aug 44
GREENHEART*	Jun 42 – Apr 43	DITCHER ᵛ	Oct 43 – Sep 44	HERMIT ᵛ	May 44 – Aug 44
MONKEYPUZZLE	Jul 42 – Aug 43	NEWSAGENT ᵛ	Oct 43 – Sep 44	SILVERSMITH ᵛ	May 44 – Sep 44
PIMENTO* ᵛ	Jul 42 – Aug 44	DIPLOMAT ᵛ	Oct 43 – Aug 44	CHANCELLOR ᵛ	Jun 44 – Sep 44
PROSPER-PHYSICIAN*	Jul 42 – Aug 44	CLERGYMAN*	Oct 43 – Aug 44	GLOVER* ᵛ	Jun 44 – Sep 44
SCIENTIST ᵛ	Jul 42 – Aug 44	GONDOLIER* ᵛ	Dec 43 – Sep 44	PERMIT ᵛ	Jul 44 – Sep 44
JUGGLER*	Jul 42 – Jan 44	FOOTMAN ᵛ	Jan 44 – Sep 44	HILLBILLY ᵛ	Jul 44 – Sep 44
BUTLER*	Jul 42 – Aug 44	LACKEY	Feb 44 – Jun 44	WOODCUTTER ᵛ	Jul 44 – Sep 44
ACROBAT*	Aug 42 – May 44	SPIRITUALIST ᵛ	Feb 44 – Aug 44	AUDITOR ᵛ	Jul 44 – Sep 44
INVENTOR*	Sep 43 – Dec 43	ORATOR*	Feb 44	LICENSEE ᵛ	Jul 44 – Sep 44
HEADMASTER* ᵛ	Sep 42 – Aug 44	SURVEYOR*	Feb 44	HELMSMAN ᵛ	Jul 44 – Aug 44
ATTORNEY	Sep 42 – Sep 43	PRIEST*	Feb 44 – Jun 44	PEDAGOGUE ᵛ	Jul 44 – Sep 44
WHEELWRIGHT ᵛ	Nov 42 – Aug 44	ACTOR ᵛ	Mar 44 – Sep 44		

Dates show when circuits were most active.

* Commander killed or capture / ᵛ Circuit survived until liberation by Allied forces

WOMEN AGENTS SENT TO FRANCE 1941–45

Codename	Real name	Section	Date of departure	
–	Giliana Gerson	DF	May 41	Returned Jun 41
MARIE	Virginia Hall	F	Aug 41	Returned Nov 42
SUZANNE	Yvonne Rudellat	F	Jul 42	Died in Belsen Apr 45
CHRISTIANE	Blanche Charlet	F	Sep 42	Arrested in Nov 42, escaped
DENISE	Andrée Borrel	F	Sep 42	Executed at Natzweiler, Jul 44
ODILE	Lise de Baissac	F	Sep 42	Returned Aug 43. (2nd mission) Apr 44 (codename MARGUERITE). Remained until liberation
ADÈLE	Marie-Thérèse le Chene	F	Oct 42	Returned Aug 43
CLAUDINE	Mary Herbert	F	Oct 42	Remained until liberation
LISE	Odette Sansom	F	Oct 42	Arrested Apr 43. Survived Ravensbrück
JACQUELINE	Jacqueline Nearne	F	Jan 43	Returned Apr 4
CLAIRE	Julienne Aisner	F	Mar 43	Returned Jun 43
MARGUERITE	Francine Agazarian	F	Mar 43	Returned Jun 43
SIMONE	Vera Leigh	F	May 43	Arrested Oct 43. Executed at Natzweiler, Jul 44
ALICE	Cecily Lefort	F	Jun 43	Arrested Sep 43. Died at Ravensbrück, 45
MADELEINE	Noor Inayat Khan	F	Jun 43	Arrested Oct 43. Executed at Dachau, Sep 44
PAULETTE	Diana Rowden	F	Jun 43	Arrested Nov 43. Executed at Natzweiler, Jul 44
ANNETTE	Yvonne Cormeau	F	Aug 43	Remained until liberation
GABY	Eliane Plewman	F	Aug 43	Arrested Mar 44. Executed at Dachau, Sep 44
MARIE	Pearl Witherington	F	Sep 43	Remained until liberation
YVONNE	Yolande Beekman	F	Sep 43	Arrested Jan 44. Executed at Dachau, Sep 44
ELIZABETH	Elizabeth Reynolds	F	Oct 43	Arrested spring 44. Liberated in prison
BINETTE	Marguerite Petitjean	RF	Jan 44	Remained until liberation
COLETTE	Anne-Marie Walters	F	Jan 44	Returned Aug 44
MAROCAIN	Danielle Redde	RF	Jan 44	Remained until liberation
PINASSE	Jeanne Bohec	RF	Feb 44	Remained until liberation
SOLANGE	Madeline Damerment	F	Feb 44	Arrested on landing. Executed at Dachau, Sep 44
AMBROISE	Denise Bloch	F	Mar 44	Arrested. Executed at Ravensbrück, 27 Jan 45
DIANE	Virginia Hall	F	Mar 44	Remained until liberation
MYRTIL	Alix d'Unenville	RF	Mar 44	Arrested, escaped and remained until liberation
ODETTE	Yvonne Baseden	F	Mar 44	Arrested Jun 44. Survived Ravensbrück
SIMONET	Patricia O'Sullivan	F	Mar 44	Remained until liberation
HÉLÈNE	Nancy Fiocca (Wake)	F	Apr 44	Remained until liberation
LOUISE	Violette Szabo	F	Apr 44	Returned Apr 44. (2nd mission) arrested Jun 44. Executed at Ravensbrück, 27 Jan 45
MIMI	Yvonne Fontaine	F	Apr 44	Remained until liberation
NADINE	Lilian Rolfe	F	Apr 44	Arrested Jul 44. Executed at Ravensbrück, 27 Jan 45
SOPHIE	Odette Wilen	F	Apr 44	Returned Aug 44
VIOLETTE	Muriel Byck	F	Apr 44	Died of meningitis in France, May 44
ALBANAIS	Marcelle Somers	RF	May 44	Remained until liberation
BLANCHE	Sonia Butt	F	May 44	Remained until liberation

GENEVIÈVE	Phyllis Latour	F	May 44	Remained until liberation
ISABELLE	Madeleine Lavigne	F	May 44	Remained until liberation. Died in Paris, Feb 45
NICOLE	Marguerite Knight	F	May 44	Remained until liberation
ADÈLE	Ginette Julian	F	Jun 44	Remained until liberation
DANUBIEN	Germaine Heim	RF	Jul 44	Remained until liberation
PAULINE	Christine Granville	F	Jul 44	Remained until liberation
VÉNITIEN	Josaine Gros	RF	Jul 44	Remained until liberation
ALTESSE	Cecile de Marcilly	RF	Aug 44	Remained until liberation
BULGARE	Eugénie Gruner	RF	Aug 44	Remained until liberation
HELLÈNE	Amiée Corge	RF	Sep 44	Remained until liberation
LANCEL	Marguerite Gianello	RF	Sep 44	Remained until liberation

FURTHER READING

Astley, J. B., & Wilkinson, P. *Gubbins and SOE* (London: Leo Cooper, 1993)

Beevor, J. G. *SOE: Recollections and Reflections 1940–1945* (London: Bodley Head, 1981)

Bell, Leslie *Sabotage: the story of Lt.-Col. J. Elder Wills* (London: T. W. Laurie, 1957)

Boyce, F., & Everett, D. *SOE: The Scientific Secrets* (Stroud: Sutton, 2003)

Braddon, R. *Nancy Wake* (London: Cassell, 1956)

Buckmaster, M. *Specially Employed* (London: Batchworth Press, 1952)

Buckmaster, M. *They fought alone: the story of British agents in France* (London: Odhams Press, 1958)

Crowdy, T. *French Resistance Fighter* (Oxford: Osprey Publishing, 2007)

Cunningham, C. *Beaulieu: the finishing school for secret agents 1941–1945* (London: Leo Cooper, 1998)

Foot, M. R. D. *SOE in France* (London: HMSO, 1966)

Foot, M. R. D. *Resistance* (London: Eyre Methuen, 1976)

Foot, M. R. D. *Six Faces of Courage* (London: Eyre Methuen, 1978)

Foot, M. R. D. *SOE: the Special Operations Executive 1940–46* (London: BBC, 1984)

Hue, A., & Southby-Tailyour, E. *The Next Moon* (London: Viking Books, 2004)

Lorain, P. *Secret Warfare: The Arms and Techniques of the Resistance* (London: Orbis Publishing, 1983)

Mackenzie, W. J. M. *The Secret History of SOE: the Special Operations Executive, 1940–1945* (London: St Ermin's, 2000)

Marks, L. *Between Silk and Cyanide: the story of SOE's code war* (London: HarperCollins, 1998)

Michel, H. (trans. Richard Barry) *The Shadow War* (London: Deutsch, 1972)

Millar, G. *Maquis* (London: Heinemann, 1945)

Public Record Office. *Operation Foxley: the British plan to kill Hitler* (Richmond: Public Record Office, 1998)

Public Record Office. *Secret agent's handbook of special devices: World War II* (Richmond: Public Record Office, 2000)

Public Record Office. *SOE syllabus: lessons in ungentlemanly warfare, World War II,* (Richmond: Public Record Office, 2001)

Stafford, D. *Secret Agent: The true story of the Special Operations Executive* (London: BBC, 2000)

INDEX